The Church
The Layman
and
The Modern World

THE MACMILLAN COMPANY
NEW YORK · CHICAGO
DALLAS · ATLANTA · SAN FRANCISCO
LONDON · MANILA

IN CANADA
BRETT-MACMILLAN LTD.
GALT, ONTARIO

The Church
The Layman
and
The Modern World

by

George H. Tavard

New York
THE MACMILLAN COMPANY
1959

Cum permissu superiorum: Rt. Rev. Henri Moquin, A.A.,
superior provincialis

Nihil obstat: Rev. Msgr. John F. Reilly,
censor deputatus

Imprimatur: ✠ Most Rev. John J. Wright,
Bishop of Worcester

The nihil obstat and imprimatur are official declarations that a book is free of error concerning Catholic faith and morals. No implication is contained therein that those who have granted the nihil obstat and imprimatur agree with the author's statements in matters of free discussion.

First Printing

Library of Congress catalog card number: 59-5988

The Macmillan Company, New York
Macmillan-Brett Ltd., Galt, Ontario

Printed in the United States of America

foreword

On a number of occasions in the past few years I have addressed audiences of lay Catholics on topics of interest to their religious life and responsibilities. Speaking to others forces you to deal with problems that otherwise would perhaps not be brought to your attention. It also incites you to explain points of view that you are unduly taking for granted. To my own advantage the audiences I had to face were on the whole critical enough to let me know what they considered weak in my views. Thus a sort of dialogue has taken place between some of our lay Catholics and myself. We have discussed the perennial meaning and the present situation of Catholic doctrine and life. When I say that this has been a dialogue, which I hope is not over, I mean to imply several points.

In the first place, although theologians may, and ought to, be better acquainted than others with the Church's official doctrine, they are not themselves the hierarchy. Their teaching is authoritative only on one condition: when it mediates, for the particular purpose of their immediate audience or reading public, the doctrine traditionally transmitted in the Church and taught by the Bishops. As for their personal standpoints,

v

the stresses they lay on one question or another, the stands they take concerning debatable matters, theologians have to take risks. They can hurt opposite opinions, cause surprise among some, meet contradiction in others. If one is willing to seek and learn, this gives rise to fruitful exchanges of views. Since I am myself in no position to speak *ex cathedra,* I can only take part in such a dialogue.

In the second place, there is a basic difficulty for a priest to write for, or speak to, laymen. For he is no longer a layman. He cannot fully share the situation of the laity. This matters little when we expound a dogmatic doctrine. For the doctrine is true independently of those to whom it is explained. It gains importance as soon as we try to appreciate moral dilemmas, psychological motivations, or spiritual ideals. We then need to smooth the sharp angles of our opinions. Catholic life can of course be described in the abstract. It cannot be lived in the abstract. It has to be lived in the various possible situations where men happen to find themselves. This must be done in constant reference to the Catholic tradition. A historical and speculative sorting out of opinions is necessary. Nevertheless one should not omit a complementary way of correcting our views: a humble study of the laity's reactions to what we write and say. For the expert is not only the scholar who knows. He is also the man who has the experience.

The present book does not claim to explain the full scope of Catholicity as it is experienced in the Church. It is neither a chapter nor a section of a treatise on Catholicism. Catholicism may be defined as the system of life and thought that flows from the Church's tradition. Catholicity will be the quality which Catholic life ingrains in those who share the Church's life. Catholicism is a surface dimension; Catholicity a depth. The present situation calls for emphasis on some aspects of

Catholicity. It makes us more sensitive to some of the constitutive elements of that Catholic quality. I have therefore
established points of contact between Catholicity and several
problems that are paramount in our time. Principles have also
been given in the light of which these problems may meet a
solution.

Some persons like to see speculative theology and immediate
problems disconnected. I have done the opposite. I have treated
both, and both together whenever possible. For I have assumed that Catholic theology is relevant to everyday life. The
theologian's vocation does not require him to sit far from the
people in the isolation of his desk. He cannot sever himself
from the human situation in his time and place. Some of the
items that are now coming to the fore in relation to the growing awareness among the Catholic laity of their theological
standing are of a speculative nature. Others arise out of the
modern predicament. The position and the solution of each
kind of problem help to posit and to solve the other kind.

This book is, in the main, addressed to laymen. An increasing
section of the Catholic laity is awake to the problems of
liturgical participation, of apostolate, of temporal responsibility. This increasing section still forms a minority. Those
who have yet to experience this awakening have missed something that rightly belongs to them. I have tried to help them
see and understand.

❊   ❊   ❊

Chapters 3, 4, and 6 were originally published in the maga-
zine *Integrity.* Their topic had been suggested by the editor,
Miss Dorothy Dohen.

Other chapters have been used for lectures.

All are indebted to persons who are too numerous to be listed here. I ought to mention, however, that Miss Joan Lorentz's assistance in the task of bringing this book into shape has been invaluable.

I finally wish to express my gratitude to the Most Reverend John J. Wright, Bishop of Worcester, for his personal interest, advice, and encouragement, in this as in other endeavors.

GEORGE H. TAVARD

ASSUMPTION COLLEGE
WORCESTER, MASS.

one

The Lay Movement

Both in its religious elements and in its secular occupations the life of a Christian is grounded in his participation in the Church's worship. The laity at prayer experiences union with Christ in the great events of the Redemption. From being a creature acknowledging the Fatherhood of God, the Church's worship transforms man into one victim with Christ. It nourishes his life as a member of the Mystical Body of God-made-man. Membership in the People of God then becomes meaningful. The Covenant passed with the Chosen People was transferred to the Church when the Jerusalem authorities failed to carry out their part of the Alliance. Since that time the Church is the messianic kingdom in process of completion. She guarantees the eventual transfiguration of the world into an everlasting city of which "God Himself and the Lamb shall be the Temple." [1] In proportion as each Christian shares the sacraments of the Church, he knows himself to be a herald of that transfiguration. He is companion to all the builders of that City, who never work in vain since God is the chief architect. The People of God, gathered around the Eucharistic

[1] Apoc. 21:22.

1

presence of the Mediator, is a "purchased people." [2] It has been purchased to go out into the lanes of the city, into the devious ways of society, along hedges and endless suburbs, there to reveal to others the strange news of what they have themselves experienced.

There are times in the history of the Church when people gain a deeper awareness of the urgency of this vocation. There are situations that draw the heart toward that persistent appeal. Such situations can sometimes be pointed at geographically and historically. Historians are acquainted with the lay movements of the Middle Ages. The best known and the most successful was no doubt the Franciscan movement. This was in origin a lay phenomenon. More than any other single influence in the thirteenth century it renovated the medieval mind. Its simplicity of lines, its stress on the essential elements of the Gospel, its discarding of forms of conventual life that tended to become unduly burdensome, its concern for spiritual freedom expressed in detachment from worldly possessions: all this was seen in the genial vision of a layman. St. Francis appealed to the common people and brought them back to what precisely constituted them as the People of God, vassals to the Great King of heaven and earth.

St. Francis inaugurated a lay movement in the fully Catholic sense of the term. Respect for the Church, for the traditional forms of her life, for her episcopal hierarchy, for her teaching: this was the very basis of his inspiration. For this reason Franciscanism stands apart among the lay movements of the Middle Ages. For most of the others were not untouched by heterodoxy. Men who were not so well balanced as Francis of Assisi were, then as now, prone to misread the human defects of the clergy as disproving the divinely instituted function of the hierarchy. Distrust of the clergy often ended with a denuncia-

[2] 1 Peter 2:9.

tion of some aspects of the Church's Institution. The conjunction of lay movements with attacks on the Church's nature reached its peak in the Protestant Reformation. When Martin Luther proclaimed the priesthood of all Christians, he repeated a traditional formula. When he opposed this general priesthood to the Eucharistic priesthood of the clergy, he emptied the formula of its intelligible contents. As often happens, the Protestant Reformation initiated a reaction that could not entirely avoid excesses. The Bishops and Popes who had to deal with the original Franciscan enthusiasm were cautious. They had reason to be. In their caution, however, they quickly discerned the ingrained fidelity of the Franciscan itinerant preachers, who were given their rightful place in the many mansions of the Church.[3] In many respects, Protestantism was also a lay movement. But it went another way. For while summoning people back to a deeper Christian life, it also questioned and discarded many traditional forms of that life. The structure of the Church was thereby threatened. Truly, the life of churchmen needs to be constantly reformed. Indeed, each faithful should every day renew his conversion to the Saviour. But the structure of the Church is grounded in a soil where reform would be meaningless: it is rooted in the Revelation of Christ given once for all. Revelation cannot be reformed.

Because they mistook the domain of human life, with its daily struggles and failures, for the domain of God's unfailing intervention in history, the Protestant Reformers provoked in the Catholic mentality of the Counter Reformation an understandable mistrust of lay movements. One cannot encourage lay movements in a period when the most influential of them

---

[3] It is true that the so-called Spiritual Franciscans were swayed by a number of heretical currents. But this was a later phenomenon in the history of the Franciscan Order.

has severed half of Europe from the Church. Catholics found themselves in a new mood when the Council of Trent shook them up. This mood was marked not only by the doctrinal intransigence which is a quality of the faith; it also favored a theological mistrust of the initiatives of laymen. One may call this overcautiousness. One can perhaps diagnose it as an unconscious shyness to which everything that looks new inspires fear. Be that as it may, theologians since that time have not excessively stressed the original status and function of the laity in the Church. Their books on the Church have tended to deal almost exclusively with her institutional framework. This was natural in so far as the Church's unambiguous condemnation of the Protestant upheaval needed explaining. It was natural. But it did not, and it could not, lead to the far-seeing, all-embracing vision that is expected of theologians.

At this point we can easily misjudge our forefathers. Yet we in a like situation would all adopt the same attitude. In their circumstances we would all have followed the same path—precisely because it was both a way back and a way ahead. After the decades of discussions and arguments that ensued on Luther's outburst, concentration on some of the essential points that Luther had questioned was a way back to constructive thinking. You cannot handle everything at once. Since the Catholic conception of the Church had been the main, if not the first, target of the Protestants, it offered the Counter Reformation a good ground to build on. Catholic theologians had to keep every item of the Catholic synthesis. They also needed, being men of their time, to take account of the new situation, and to answer the questions raised by their contemporaries. St. Thomas had focused his system on the return of all things to God. His post-Reformation disciples gradually made the Church as Institution the center of their thought.

This was also a way ahead out of an apparent dilemma. Nobody could know it at the time. Yet subsequent happenings have thrown light on the wisdom of such a concentration on ecclesiology. When you expound the structure of the Church, you naturally highlight the meaning, the function, and the prerogatives of the hierarchy. This emphasis may bypass the people itself for whose salvation the Church exists. Yet no deadlock follows. In the nature of things, the dilemma, if there be one, will be short-lived. With no theological revolution, without disregarding the efforts of the last centuries, modern ecclesiologists have restored the laity to their place in the theological tractates on the Church. What has happened is this. The Church according to Catholic doctrine is both an earthly society and the Mystical Body of Christ. This implies that if you concentrate on either aspect of the Church's nature, you sooner or later pierce through to the other. The theologians who centered their reflection on the Institution of the Church smoothed the way for those who, pursuing their thought in its innate direction, would see the Institution as the Event of Christ's presence among us. In the history of ecclesiological research, we are now exactly at the point where the Institution of the Church as a society leads to the Mystical Body of Christ by way of their mutual identity.

However short it has to be, a historical account of ecclesiology throws light, I believe, on the nature and destiny of the present lay movement. Modern theologians stress an old truth: the laity is not a passive mass on which the hierarchy may exercise authority. It is, rather, an active membership in the Mystical Body of Christ, in the People of God announcing the coming of the City of God. Through much more than a mere coincidence, our age is also marked by what may well be the first important lay movement since the sixteenth century, and the first fully Catholic one since the thirteenth. I do not wish to treat of this here in systematic fashion. For what is a sum of loosely connected endeavors should not be erected into a system.

Unlike its predecessors in the past, the modern lay movement cannot be defined in terms of a definite objective or of a dominant mentality. It owes its inception to no particular figure. Its manifestations take many forms. This vagueness or lack of contours is itself significant. One can account for it: the modern lay movement represents no less than a major stage in the historical development of the Church. At a time when education was, owing to circumstances, all but reserved to the clergy, and to only a part of the clergy at that, the hierarchy normally assumed functions that do not of themselves belong to its evangelical mission. Hospitals, pawnshops, universities were created by the clergy. With the increasing education of larger masses of people, it is equally normal that more and more of these extra charges should pass from the clergy to the laity. With the modern extension of technical knowledge, it is now the clergy itself which, compared to many sections of the laity, is underinstructed. From this point of view, the access of the Catholic laity to responsibility in fields that were formerly clerical reserves corresponds to a sociological necessity.

There is, however, much more than this at stake. In the domain of liturgical participation, as in that of the apostolate, growing fractions of the Catholic laity are more and more aware of their specific possibilities. The time when the laity was satisfied with passive assistance at church seems to be, from a number of symptoms, on the way out. The organized liturgical movements of several countries witness to this. The hierarchy has listened with friendliness to the voice of liturgical congresses and has inaugurated liturgical modifications: the sense of the Church points in that direction. Not all countries have reached the same point of development. Not all national liturgical movements feel an equal degree of concern. For the laity does not everywhere undergo the same pressure from external causes.

Likewise for the laity's participation in the apostolate. It is everywhere accepted that the layman is called on to spread the faith. A basic dogmatic proviso adds that only in subordination to the hierarchy can he contribute to this extension of the Church. In the words of a recent papal document, "there never was, there is not and there shall never be in the Church a legitimate magisterium of laymen that would be exempted by God from the authority, the guidance and the watchfulness of the sacred magisterium." The contrary assumption would be "the symptom and the fruit of a spiritual disease." Once this disease has been prevented, the laity's call to the apostolate is a sign of health in the body of the Church. It "deserves the greatest praises and must be energetically developed." [4] How this can be done in practice varies from area to area. Not only will methods differ. Some underlying concepts may also be far from coterminous. The notion of Catholic Action does not evoke quite the same connotations, say, in Eire and in Germany. The secular background of the two nations has tainted Catholic sensibilities to a point where they cannot face their problems with one reaction—to say nothing of the fact that the problems themselves are not identical.

There may be a significant difference between the European lay movement and its American counterpart. This matter would need longer study than can be made here. We therefore do not intend to reach any definite conclusion. Yet trends are sufficiently clear on both sides of the Atlantic to allow us to draw a tentative sketch of the situation. The distinction in question should not be overstressed: it is not a difference of nature.

[4] Address of May 31, 1954, to an audience of Cardinals and Bishops.

In either case there are Catholic laymen who try to develop a properly lay spirituality, taking full account of their situation as laymen, yet opening into an active participation in the tasks of the Church.

A basic difference lies, however, in the original incentive at work. In European countries the laity has been used, by the nature of the national traditions in which it lives, to consider the Church as a social power of major importance. This has even led to deviations, as in the left-wing exaggerations of Le Sillon or the right-wing excesses of L'Action Française. Yet whether people like it or not, the European way of life has evolved out of a civilization that was directly Catholic. From the Middle Ages to our day the continuity is traceable in spite of upheavals and revolutions. On this background, the process of emancipation whereby political adulthood was slowly reached has a correspondent in the development of a responsible laity, in what we may call the secularization of the apostolate. When Pius XI called competent laymen to "participate in the apostolate of the hierarchy," he introduced no novelty. He simply recognized a fact. The clergy had from time to time abandoned to laymen some of the social functions it used to perform. The time was now ripe and the circumstances were favorable to take another step: under the hierarchy the laity could assume part of the task for which the hierarchy has exclusive responsibility. This came at the acme of a long development. Pius XI effected no reversal of values. He said only that the laity had matured enough to exploit its apostolic virtualities to the full. The incentive ultimately came, I should think, from the laity. Through successes and reverses, through wars, revolutions, and peace, through the Industrial Revolution and social unrest, the Catholic laity of Europe had clung to the continuity of the Church amid a changing social order. It now remained to reinterpret the same social order and its evolution with an apostolic rather than with a social motivation, and to transform it with the leaven of the Catholic faith.

In a country where the Church has had to start from scratch and, in less than a century, to become a huge organization on the scale of a vast continent, the lay movement cannot exhibit the same features. The "specialized" Catholic Action of Pius XI better fitted the European situation, out of which it arose, than the American scene. At the mid-century it has not yet been grafted onto America with outstanding success. This is not necessarily to be regretted. For if we are soundly realistic we must admit that some methods and mentalities cannot be successfully exported. In this instance a relative failure was to be expected. For the American Catholic layman of this day is not the product of centuries of a family tradition that has remained continuous throughout its growth. More or less distant in his past there has been the uprooting of emigration, followed by a new start in a country nurtured from the beginning by Protestant culture. The American layman has not little by little assumed functions that the clergy had undertaken before. In the first place, the clergy, with a few brilliant exceptions, has never been in a socially dominant position. In the second, the laity was too long concerned with economic survival to be able to fulfill more than minimum religious obligations.

There is nonetheless a lay movement in twentieth century America. Its strength does not lie, I would suggest, in parish sodalities. These are under close clergy supervision, whereas a lay movement is, by definition, headed by laymen. Lay societies on the national plane, of which the Knights of Columbus provides the pattern, also fall short of qualifying for leadership in the lay movement. For neither their aims nor their methods are directly apostolic.

The American lay movement, at the present stage of its development, is unorganized. It is made of small, informal groups loosely connected by their reading of Catholic lay periodicals like *Jubilee* or *Commonweal*. It exists in the exact measure in which sound theology has become available to the laity. It grows with this education. In other words, the lay movement in the United States is not yet marked, as in Europe, by a special method of evangelization, the apostolate to laymen by laymen of the same milieu. It is rather characterized by a strong desire for a deeper, more vital, more existential grasp of the Catholic faith. An aspiration to action will follow this better knowledge of, and more immediate concern with, the teaching and the life of the Church. If the European lay movement tends to increase and to multiply apostolic endeavors, its American counterpart may be viewed as developing the Catholic dimension in the life of the Catholic laity.[5]

Being mainly of sociological origin, this difference does not call for judgment. It is good, however, to know the facts. Only thus may we hope to promote the laity in the way that will prove the most useful to the entire Church. It could be shown with considerable probability that European forms of the lay apostolate cannot easily be installed in the United States. However valuable they may be in their home countries, they have been marked by the society in which they were born. The American pattern requires something else. Whether or not the changing structures of American society will sooner or later present suitable ground for this is a moot question that may not be answered now without intemperate guessing. At any rate it would seem more convenient, in the long run, not to wait for such a transformation to be over. The lay movement

[5] Yet the desire for action opens the mind to its need of more knowledge. Thus many Bible-study groups in French circles have stemmed out of Catholic Action.

that is being born now needs to be assisted precisely as it stands. The specific forms that it will adopt when contemplation turns into action will take shape of themselves when the time is ripe. This is not to say that no American group is actively engaged in apostolic work. There are such lay groups. But if we try to characterize the movement as a whole, it is clear that these groups do not at present dominate the pattern.

The two aspects of the modern lay movement may actually be successive phases in one development. European Catholics of the last century multiplied educational institutions and organizations, thus making possible the lay apostolate of the recent decades. The present concern in America over better religious instruction and the recurrent clamor for a theology for the layman may also, in their turn, forerun a Catholic Action of tomorrow.

two

The Catholic Community

The idea of a community is that of a home. Yet homes are of two kinds. One of these is made of bricks, wood, stones, or concrete. It connotes the souvenirs, dreams, or ambitions attaching to the places where we have lived happily. The other sort of home everyone tries to build around himself: it is made of human beings united in a community of friendship.

The material home is linked to a particular place. The community binds us to particular persons. It is a home made of living beings in whose company we feel as much at ease, as peaceful as in the surroundings of our material home. But the peace then attained belongs to another level of experience. Instead of being psychological, it is spiritual. The spiritual nature of the community is even, in the case of the family, sanctified by a sacrament.

In the Catholic tradition the family is not (however much its sacredness must be stressed) the highest kind of spiritual community. Even when it has been made holy by the sacrament, a family can remain closed in upon itself in a barren collective selfishness. When this happens, it is usually the child who saves the family by breaking out of it, by forming ties with others and thus forcing the limited family community to open itself to outsiders. Hence the rise of neighborhood communities. The mutual relationships of these dovetailing communities form the object of the art of politics, on the local, national, and international levels.

A danger lurks around the formation of these necessary secular communities: many Catholics have gradually forgotten that their family is included in a praying community. Emphasis on praying together in the home is excellent, up to the point when the family considers itself to be *the* Catholic community of prayer. When this takes place, the family has once more closed itself. This time it has not only shut out individuals, neighbors, or strangers; it has also tried to substitute itself for the Church. It has renounced the dimension of Catholicity that can be reached only in the praying community of the Church.

The praying community is the Church, the whole Church. On the local plane it is, likewise, the whole Church as present and gathered together in one place—in Corinth or Ephesus at the time of St. Paul, in Toledo or Omaha in our own day. It is made of all who live in a given area and to whom the glad tidings of Redemption have been made known in baptism. What they share is wider than any single person or any single family, wider than any single national or racial group. It is no less than the totality of Revelation, than the common presence of Christ with His disciples. This is why the parish (which is no other than the Church as a neighborhood praying community) has three basic characteristics. It is *territorial*, open to all in its area and not to one linguistic or social group only. It is *liturgical*, gathered in the common experience of the liturgy where it makes visible the Mystical Body of Christ. It is *missionary*, destined to summon in and welcome all men in its territory, just as the Church as a whole is destined to bring all mankind to the Gospel.

On paper, the parish is all this. In practice, the last two aspects are sometimes largely non-existent. Many Catholic communities have gradually lost track of their liturgical obligations. These are not met once a Sunday Mass has been ensured to those who can invest a dime in the entrance collection box. Nor are most parishes geared to tackle the huge problem of non-Catholic praying communities in their area. As for the territorial principle, how many priests can visit all their territory? And how many laymen go to another Church that happens to be nearer?

It is clear enough that, without it being necessarily a catastrophe, the parish has now broken down as the praying and missionary community of the People of God in a given area.

The kind of society we live in is largely responsible for that.

Due attention should be paid to the fact that every search for a community is implicitly religious. Man is a social animal. This is not traceable to some herd instinct that may have been inherited from prehuman ancestors. It is not because he needs to associate with others in order to be strong or efficient. (Great geniuses, who in this or that field are precisely more human than others, have always been isolated.) The actual reason is this: man is haunted by the fact that God's life is a community life. Man senses this whether God's life is known to him through Jesus Christ, or imperfectly described by the prophets of non-Christian religions, or only dimly perceived in his soul. Whether he knows it or not, every man who longs to be with men pays tribute to the Blessed Trinity. The more inclusive and spiritual the fellowship he desires, the nearer he is to God. Our age boasts of atheism. Yet there is ground to think that it is more religious than it knows. To no meager extent, its atheistic claim makes our century paradoxically God-centered. For it negates notions of God that do not seem worthy of a Being who would be pure fellowship. There are men whose "religion" is proportionate to their atheism in the sense that they entertain a higher idea of the glory of God than would-be religious persons whose conception of God debases Him. Implicit forms of the love of God deserve respect. They herald a better future for the ultimate community of God's love, the Catholic Church.

The communities we have built or that are being built around us are nonetheless far from religious. The greatest nations, both the most powerful in terms of economic or military strength and the most influential in terms of culture, are avowedly indifferent to religion. Here again there is something highly though hiddenly religious in seeking the temporal good of all men just because they share the same human nature, without reference to their religious beliefs. To respect man means to revere God. Giving a man a glass of water, we lend it to Christ. Yet the natural weight of a purely secular society slowly drives it to idolatry. It tends to take the place of God. The modern tendency to totalitarianism, which is felt in democracies as well as in dictatorships, is a potent illustration of this.

The mill, factory, store, office, and the sundry environments of man's work, the working communities of an industrial civilization, are also the products of a nonreligious secularism. More than anything else they have wrecked the scope of the parish as community. They have torn man from his family and his neighborhood, where the professional side of him usually remains a stranger. His family and neighborhood have also become strangers to his work. His presence at Church tends to become an occasional phrase between brackets thrown into the course of a long sentence dealing with something else. It may be a sideline like the various hobbies that man enjoys once in a while. Yet here again his job makes him one with many others: one in a production chain or along an assembly belt where thousands of others are at work. Every movement harmoniously fits in the sum total of all other movements. Man thus acts in a para-liturgy which at worst apes and at best reflects the God-given order of the universe. There is thus a religious opening in the fellowship of work, if one only knows it, if one is not too tired or too hungry or too doped or too disillusioned to be aware of it. Yet this is only an implicit form of the love of God. It is not yet the community of the children of God.

I am not certain that we should regret the mushroom growth of nonreligious communities. For in some more or less remote areas the former pattern has subsisted. The parish church stands as the true community center. Life is regulated by the church bells. The pastor is the most influential person in the locality. This is still so in parts of Brittany, Eire, or Canada. I should imagine it was like that till recently in sections of Poland or Lithuania. And the result is not altogether satisfactory. Instead of leading the world, these islands fight against it a losing battle. In their determination they do not notice that what they wish to stave off is sometimes excellent. Examples abound of cases where the struggle to preserve morality has taken little account of the demands of charity or justice. Fear of God, as Scripture says, is the beginning of wisdom. But men and women to whom the Church has entrusted her sacraments and her doctrine are not supposed to be content with only the beginning of wisdom. A world outlook that does not fear to face the enormous amount of evil let loose in the world is one of the elements that make Christianity mature. In the past state of Christendom the religious community had predominance over all others. The remains of that Christendom now form the rear guard of the Church militant instead of being its vanguard.

Here and there experiments in parish life on the part of

pioneers have tried to restore the parish as the Catholic community in the midst of modern environment. Some emphasize its missionary aspects, as is done by Abbé Michonneau in his famous Sacré-Cœur de Colombes near Paris. Others, like the late Abbé Remilleux in Lyons, develop the liturgical aspect first. These efforts may eventually solve the problem of the religious community in one spot. They will create *in their area* a real Christian community of *prayer* and *witness* (the three characteristics of the parish) organically connected with the working and neighborhood communities of the area. As long as the effort remains isolated, however, such an organic connection cannot be perfect.

The parish of modern times needs therefore to develop its Catholicity. This should not consist only in membership in the Roman Catholic Church. It is good to bear the name of Catholic. Yet a nominal Catholicism is far from the ideal of Catholicity that is proposed by the very nature of the Church. Catholicism may be seen as a system of thought and a way of life. Individuals and communities can structurally belong to it. They have adopted what Pope Pius XII called its "ideological system." Their allegiance is given to it. Within this framework, however, the possibility remains of letting the seed of Catholicity grow sterile. In the words of Pius XII: "The expression 'Catholicism' . . . is neither usual with, nor fully adequate to, the Church. She is much more than a mere ideological system. . . . She is a truly living organism." [1] One can believe Catholicism as an "ideological system," yet fall short of full participation in the life of the Church as a "living organism." Catholicity is precisely this dimension of depth and this power of life within Catholicism. A community grows into Catholicity only by focusing all its life on the doings of the universal Church

[1] Discourse to the 10th International Congress of Historical Sciences, Sept. 7, 1955.

throughout the world and on the spiritual needs of men in all their implications. It thus develops what may be called a horizontal and a vertical Catholicity. Everything in such a community is centered on the essence of the liturgy: this increases its Catholicity in a vertical direction. It also pivots around the nature and scope of the Christian's mission in the world: this ensures a horizontal progress of Catholicity.

There was a time when a layman was judged a good Catholic if he knew the Apostles' Creed, the Lord's Prayer, and the Ten Commandments.[2] Such a standard would be satisfactory today on the part of the mentally underdeveloped. As a keystone of religious culture among the laity it would be appallingly inadequate. But since grace builds upon nature, a religious culture supposes a human culture. At each of its levels, therefore, the Catholic community has to be a center of human and theological culture no less than of worship. This applies to the parish as to every other type of Catholic community. The ideal would be attained if they could grow into thinking centers. People of all persuasions are today looking for an intelligent philosophy of life that can account for the civilization that we have developed. They long to exchange and compare experiences and outlooks. Clerical censorship is, admittedly, irksome to the modern mind. Yet experience shows that a theological guidance is welcome when it is truly directed toward the problems of our society and time. Anything, a public event, a book, a talk, or even a movie, can lead to a vital discussion, since every human experience implicitly moots the ultimate question: What is the meaning of existence? The ultimate answer is given in the Revelation of Christ as communicated through the Church. It still has to be proposed to each man as the response to his existential query.

[2] As late as 1523 the Franciscan theologian Caspar Schatzgeyer held this to be sufficient for men who are not entrusted with care of souls. (Cf. his *Examen Novarum Doctrinarum,* assertio 97.)

Children contribute to open a parish on its neighborhood. For schools and playgrounds are usually not strictly parochial. Men and women can open it on the world of business by carrying the Gospel with them to work. The current disconnectedness between working life and religious life nevertheless still needs to be overcome. This is no easy task. Each man belongs to two sorts of environment at least, his locality and his work. In these conditions it may be necessary to develop a twofold system of religious communities. The parish remaining the geographic unit, something else may also claim men from the standpoint of their vocational occupation. Many sodalities and Catholic Action groups work on that basis. This may have to be enlarged into a regular feature of popular Catholic culture. Yet this should be done without overstressing the institutional aspect of this secondary community. Institutions tend to cool off into self-complacent organizations. They need to be reminded that we have no permanent city here below. We have only tents that can be pitched at night and folded up at dawn when the caravan of life moves on. Thus no one sort of manmade community should try to outlive the span of time through which it can bear fruit in the shifting pattern of society.

The parish community is meant to be the total Catholic Church in a given area. Organisms that are not on a local basis contribute to its life as it does to that of individuals. This openness on others is part of Catholicity. Deprived of it, no community could be the Christian nerve cell transmitting to the whole body of the world the inspiration and the power of the Revelation in Christ.

Like everything human, the requirements of a modern parish evolve. Their details lie outside of our topic. But since we deal with the local Catholic community as the incarnational unit of Revelation in society, we are interested in the principles of such an evolution. Creative imagination needs to be controlled when it is applied to the development of Christian life. Yet without this creative imagination, everything would freeze into a permanent stalemate. Now two opposite dangers threaten those who are concerned with developing a really Catholic community life.

The first danger, presumably the more common in America, would be to attempt a restoration of the classical type of parish. This type supposed a society patterned by Catholicism itself as an "ideological system." It flourished in the past. We see outdated remains of it everywhere. Our pluralistic society makes such a restoration totally unthinkable. For it would have to be effected in opposition to sociological trends that do not seem to be reversible. This is the acknowledged or unconscious temptation of the most conservative. The risk is serious. It can give non-Catholics the wrong impression that the Church is a reactionary force trying to stem the march of time.

The second danger is also frequent. It despairs of the principle of the parish community. Then one rests content with the basically secular communities into which men are grouped for work. That these may be, as we have seen, implicitly religious does not help matters at this point. For the implicitly religious has to be made explicit. And this can only be done in the Church. Not a few of the French priest-workers fell into this excess. Were the idea carried out to its logical end, it would mean discarding altogether the principle of a Christian community as a community of prayer and witness. The parish must be organically connected with all legitimate secular communities. This is required by its nature and for its survival. Yet it should remain itself the missionary house of prayer. It cannot become or supplant the factory any more than it can replace the family. It can neither be absorbed by the factory nor entirely disappear before the family.

What the Church is in the universe the local Catholic community should strive to be within its limits. The Church respects all economic planning and all political measures that respect man. She condemns all that contemn man. The local Catholic community likewise has to respect human relationships that are not explicitly religious, as long as they promote the temporal good of man.

Emerging from the depths of the liturgical mystery, she will then carry the message of Christ to the most unexpected street corner and the dirtiest office building. She is the Catholic Church, where the smallest as well as the greatest carry the burden of the whole; the Apostolic Church, where all are sent to the unbelieving world, led by the successors of the Apostles; the Church militant and triumphant, where each is the light of the world because he shares with all others the fire of the Holy Spirit; the little flock that knows no fear because it has been promised a Kingdom.

three

In a
Technological World

The Christmas message of Pope Pius XII for 1953 denounced the technological society, in all its forms, as basically unchristian. Yet men have to be Christian where they happen to be living. Do what they will, a good number cannot escape from the dominion of technics. They must coexist with technology long enough to transform it. It is true that many, Catholic or not, have simply yielded to technological standards. They are happy with the present form of capitalism. They simply want to enjoy it and, as much as possible, to sanctify it with good intentions. Others have revolted. "Distributism" has been proposed as a way out. But, whatever its theoretical merits, there is ground to think that it has failed as a way of life for the average man. It has not even been tried. Perhaps it could not be tried. At any rate, the implication of both positions is that we ought to be either "for" or "against" technics. Yet there are few "either-or" situations in life. And there is no compelling reason to assume that this is one of them. What is needed first is a deeper reflection on the human situation.

The problem of technology is not exactly new. Because the scholastics were aware of it they commonly began their "Books of Sentences" (the encyclopedias of their time) with a discussion of the nature and the mutual relationships of *frui* (enjoyment) and *uti* (use). For modern readers this may be translated: interpretation and usage, contemplation and skill, beauty and utility, theology and technics. Must we give primacy to methods of interpretation, like craftsmanship, art, philosophy, religion, or to techniques of dominion over nature, like the applied sciences of production, circulation, and consummation? This is, at bottom, the question that technology posits.

Roughly speaking, our civilization has passed from the first to the second emphasis. The Middle Ages gave pride of place to a religious interpretation of man, to which all else was subordinate. In today's United States the study of the market and advertising are all-important. The values of exchange have eclipsed all others. This constitutes the extreme kind of the second type. The Soviet Union seems to be a mixed type: it stresses production values, but in close connection with a particular philosophical theory, Marxism. Western Europe in general also represents a mixed type. Some areas and classes place values of interpretation on top. Others are dominated by the production-exchange cycle. Several interpretations, especially Christian, Marxist, and existentialist, are in conflict, though they all tend to oppose, on varying grounds, the business-dominated circles.

These emphases have baneful consequences. An overstress on the primacy of interpretation creates a theocratic society. The deity involved may be Yahweh, Allah, Tao, Bramah, the ultimate of this or that school of thought or even, as in some political philosophies at the end of the Middle Ages, the Papacy. But whatever—it ends in a nonprogressive sort of society. It is doomed to decay as soon as the yardstick adopted ceases to fit the needs of men. On the other hand, overemphasis on the primacy of business enslaves man to production or to money.

It ushers in the reign of the Superman, the man who produces all he wants and enjoys all he can.

In both cases we must protest in the name of Christianity. For Christ came to free us from "the traditions of man" and from "the elemental powers of the world." These may be paraphrased: the too human philosophies of life, and the cult of power and money. Christ has liberated us. "The spiritual man judges all things and he is judged by no one." [1] The trouble is that we have only the seed of the spiritual man, at a more or less retarded degree of growth. The problem of how to be a Christian in this world is therefore twofold. We must behave "spiritually." Yet we must be humble enough to acknowledge the bondage to matter and to society of that part of us which is not yet liberated. Or, to look at it from another angle, we must submit to society and to matter up to the point where we are mature enough to "judge all things." This point is set in the eternal life, when we are resurrected from the dead. Christians here on earth belong to an intermediate stage. Their freedom of contemplation must be rooted in service, in obedience to the technics that keep society going. Service finds its meaning in freedom. A Christian society would not impose more technology than men can take. It would progress, thanks to the free service of those who are spiritual enough to be immerged in technics without overlooking their meaning.

The Christian man, thus described, does not escape from technology and "go back to the land" where he may perchance forget modern gadgets. Nor does he seek paradise in the buying power of his dollars. The paradise of the latter would be an opiate. It would hide the God-given value of creation. And the refuge of the former cannot be shared by all. Yet the true paradise must be within reach of every man. And it must be open to a spiritual interpretation. A Christian social order

[1] 1 Cor. 2:15.

would therefore not consist in reverting to the family spinning wheel. Nor would it force everybody into a superplant. Formerly Christians could give a sense to the spinning wheel. Today or tomorrow the Christian interpretation must give a purpose to the superplant. A Christian society for our time must assume all the technics developed in the last centuries. It must accept every single item of this man-made scientific tradition and every social responsibility that this entails. But all must be imbued with the tremendous transfiguring power of the Spirit of God. This means reaching a balance between ways of interpretation and technics of utilization. To be a Christian in technological society one needs a spiritual insight that must be the deeper as technics are the more advanced.

A huge effort should be made before we reach this balance. As it is commonly presented, the Christian interpretation of the world, be it Catholic or Protestant, is not on a level with technics of production, comfort, and fun. An amazing amount of imagination is poured into pioneering ways of enjoying life. How little imagination is put at the service of the Church can meanwhile be gauged any day by reading Catholic "literature" or listening to Catholic speakers. The mind that explains the catechism and the one that runs a factory have not been measured on the same scale. The latter is a master of technique. The former has at its disposal the fullness of Revelation, but fails to make it a living and telling message. There is no bridge from the one to the other. Such a bridge is yet to be built.

There are many aspects to this. Take, for instance, the problem of the family. We are reminded here and there that before restoring society, one must restore the home; before developing a Christian art on a large scale, one must form a family art at home. Sanctity in the home will sanctify society: is not society a collection of homes? Yet this is too simple to be true. The family is admittedly the basic social unit. A well ordered society is patterned on its needs. Yet in practice the destiny of the family and that of the city where it lives are necessarily intertwined. An urban family that would be indifferent to the welfare of its city would hardly be Christian. The Christian family accepts the responsibility of living here and now. It willingly shares the destiny of those who have no choice but to live here and now. Once we choose to live in a slum, it is no longer a slum in the full sense. Loving acceptance of necessity marks the beginning of redemption. For then there is necessity no longer. "Where the Spirit of Christ is, there is liberty."[2] A family cannot be Christian unless it also christianizes society. There is no antecedence of the one to the other.

Or take the intellectuals. Because they have been complacent, few Christians have attempted in earnest to introduce into Christian culture the insights of modern artists (whether cubist painters or jazz players) and those of modern thinkers (whether Karl Marx or Jean-Paul Sartre). There is of course no more question of swapping plain chant for New Orleans blues than there is of giving up St. Thomas for Heidegger. But neither Heidegger nor Louis Armstrong may find his ultimate meaning as long as he is cut off from plainsong and Aquinas. This is a task that only Christians are equipped to do. Yet how many Catholic universities have taken St. Thomas seriously enough to find out on what points he did not claim to say the last words? In connection with this, much has been written lately on the supposedly various brands of Catholicism. Is the "adolescent American Church" distinct from the "ancient Christianity" of Europe? Is there an "oceanic," or new, and a "Continental," or old, Catholicism? The question is artificial. Superficially speaking, Catholicism in each land is molded in the distinct sociologi-

[2] 2 Cor. 3:17.

cal patterns of each country. To some extent it has been marked
by distinct cultures. This is normal and healthy. One may like
or dislike the pattern in question. One may, usually one should,
try to better it. Yet there is no ultimate difference here. In final
analysis the only far-reaching distinction is between those who
see and those who do not see the points where Christianity can
find a place in modern culture. It is abnormal that there should
be some who do not perceive this. In fact they seem to form a
majority. But this distinction of two Catholicisms is not geo-
graphical; it crosses all national boundaries.

Every society posits questions to the man who lives in it.
Sooner or later man seeks for an answer. Art attempts to em-
body the question and, sometimes, to hint at an answer. Philosophy tries to do it in another idiom. In their own language,
depth psychology and sociology endeavor, as the case may be,
to explain the whole thing away or to throw light on the situation where the question arises. The problem is as old as the
world, yet it is always being formulated anew. It is the problem
of life and death, of joy and sorrow, in a word, of existence.
The ultimate answer cannot be found outside the Revelation in
Christ. Yet there is plenty of food for thought in the frequent
sneers of some Catholics at modern painting, music, philosophy,
depth psychology, and other expressions of the contemporary
mind. From the height of their all-embracing wisdom, self-
appointed spokesmen see, judge, and anathematize. They even
seem to be surprised that abstract painters, jazz enthusiasts, ex-
istentialists, and all varieties of psychoanalysts do not listen
to them. No wonder: these men seek for an answer in a language
they know. Misunderstanding provides no answer. It only ignores the question. On the contrary, Christianity becomes relevant when it helps posit the question and when it proposes an
answer in a comprehensible idiom. This cannot be done if

Christians escape the technological society. Nor can it be done if they are so happy with it that the anxiety of modern man becomes meaningless for them.

An important side issue ought to be mentioned. Not every society is yet dominated by technology. There are still fortunate parts of every continent where the technics in use have remained proportionate to the current philosophy of life. In our self-congratulating parlance we call them "backward." Modern communications, however, have brought them into contact with industrial man. Thus the frontier where Americans pioneer now covers half the world. This gives American Christians a new responsibility. For the needs of defense or for those of business, we are introducing technological patterns of life to so-called underdeveloped areas. For pious purposes we call this bringing "civilization" to "savages." The Catholic, as well as the secular, press is openly gleeful about it. Yet this is where we are sowing the wind for others to reap the storm. It is inhuman, and therefore immoral, to introduce to technology peoples whose interpretation of life has no room for it. Technics of utilization should not outrun spirituality, or else we prepare among others the split between daily life and religion of which we ourselves suffer. Thus there is a crisis in the Arab soul: the Koran provides no adequate interpretation of industrialism. What kind of future are we looking forward to when we urge industrialization on the Moslem world? Africa is in a dilemma: the tribal traditions are unrelated to the modernity of the intellectuals who lead nationalist movements. Can we simply hail the nationalists as liberators and forget about the tribesmen?

This is probably the greatest sin of modern technology. It covers the whole world little by little, regardless of the human element on which it leaves its mark. This is also its greatest victory over Christianity. For it has converted most Christians to its aims. There follows a challenge for men who accept the responsibility of being modern while trying to be faithful also to the Gospel. They have to check this invasion of the souls of men and the consequent disruption of other types of civilization. "Backward" areas, so called, should themselves develop their own pattern of modernity, keeping interpretation on a par with exploitation. To judge from the tone of the press when speaking of colonial countries, very few seem to be aware of this human problem.

Naturally it may be objected that while all this is fine and true, it is not for the man in the street. An élite may perhaps raise the world of technics to its spiritual meaning. It may be able to keep happy proportions between humanity and necessity. As for the unsophisticated man, he is simply left with a plain choice: for or against, slavery or escape, technology or, at his level, theology. But this is not correct. For when He likened his followers to a leaven, Christ obviously intended to make them into an élite. They are one indeed, if only they realize that they cannot save themselves while letting the rest of the world go hang. No one can say, with Cain, "Am I my brother's keeper?" When a Christian is satisfied with the reign of technology, with deep-freezers, supermarkets, throughways, and supersonic planes, he is a traitor. There is no room for Christ if technology fulfills the needs of man. We do not need to be saved if technics have redeemed us. We do not have to continue our pilgrimage if we have arrived. Yet if he is so dissatisfied that he hankers for some past stage in the evolution from the cave man to the space traveler, the Christian is a traitor too. For Christ is to be announced in every environment and civilization. If one cannot be a Christian in a technological environment, we may all turn Marxist, for we have nothing to lose. The conditions of production make the man, both for the Marxist and for the Christian who despairs of his century. The Christian for whom technics cannot be redeemed is not a thoroughgoing Christian.

A warning also needs to be given to the other side. The man for whom technology is above redemption cannot be a Christian at all. He has fallen a prey to efficiency. He believes in a revelation through factory sirens and the shuffle of the assembly-line belt. In his Christmas message for 1954, Pius XII referred to the efficaciousness of Marxism, "based on a false idea, an idea, moreover, violating primary human and divine rights, yet at the same time efficacious." A society may work, yet on a wrong basis. Truth is not measured by success. It matters little if the success in question is hailed in a booming stock market or by the teams that carry out a five-year plan. Besides, we have only to read about history and we shall see that efficiency is clearly not one of the marks of the Church. A Christian trusts neither the capitalist nor the communist efficiency. He believes in the power of God.

The question of John Dos Passos in *1919*, "Where do we go from here, boys? Where do we go from here?" is being repeated on all keys around us. The tremendous technical development of our age gives the question a sharper edge than it ever had before. It is our task to answer it, the task of the Catholic laity. Some may say: "We have the answer. We have all the answers. And everybody knows it. Or if they don't, they just have to ask us." The point is, nobody will ask us, if we give him the impression that we do not belong to his world. I have before my eyes a speech that was made at Evanston, Illinois, in August, 1954, by Professor Joseph Hromadka, a Protestant theologian from Czechoslovakia. Whatever the merits or demerits of Hromadka's political alliances, I cannot resist quoting him. What he says is very relevant here: "There is no darkness, no corruption, no wretchedness, no sin, no misery and destitution that can prevent God from being, in His gracious love and compassion, present exactly where no man would dare to expect him. . . . To believe in Jesus Christ is to be where He is and does His work, to be on His side in His continuous struggle with human sin and suffering, with injustice and death, with bigotry and selfishness, with pride and religious self-assurance." The prosperous capitalist does not save the world by going to Mass on Sunday. He rather saves the world of business if he "buys as though not owning." [3] The would-be radical does not save the world by turning his back to the machine. He rather saves the world of labor if he freely shares the destiny of those who are tied down to the machine because they have no choice. The Christian of Poland or China does not save his country when he adopts Communist standards. But he contributes to transform Marxism if he gives up out of love the part of liberty that others renounce out of fear. For all then unite their human situation with its Christian interpretation. They thus prepare the ground for a transformation of the secular reality under the impact of faith and love.

We can neither stay where we are nor return to happier times. We can only go forward to a new Christendom, where religion and technics shall not be indifferent or hostile to each other.

[3] 1 Cor. 7:30.

four
Freedom and
Authority

Most of the modern movements for freedom have ended by establishing tyranny. This was true of the French as it still is of the Russian revolution. In South America the republics freed from Spanish rule are more often than not in the hands of "strong men." The North American settlers achieved a revolution that did not end in tyranny. Yet their concept of liberty did not apply equally well to Indians and to Negroes. And it remains to be seen if the emancipation of colonial countries in our own day will be a change for the better, in respect to the independence enjoyed by the average man. This may mean that achievements fall short of ideals. It may also imply that the modern notion of freedom is self-destroying.

In the field of religion, historians know that those who fought most for liberty for their own interpretation of Christianity were the very ones who forced their beliefs on everyone else. Calvin disapproved of the Inquisition when the Inquisition condemned him. He was disposed to collaborate with inquisitors in hunting down Michael Servetus. Is religious liberty then also an ambiguous concept?

The New Testament has something to say about liberty that

sounds strange in our day. "The truth shall make you free." [1]
Christ, Who is the truth, is also the way and the life. Spiritual
liberation from the devil and the world is achieved in a life that
follows the way of truth taught by Christ. The truth taught by
Christ is Himself: the mystery of the Cross, the identification,
in Him, of the Absolute and the Crucified. Translated in
ethical terms, it is the Sermon on the Mount: blessedness for
those who weep. Both as dogma and as morals, the truth of
Christianity is paradoxical. Like the Resurrection that gives it
substance, it is "stumbling-block to Jews, foolishness to Gen-
tiles." [2] For here liberation, freedom are valid concepts only
in relation to an absolute, to the truth which Christ is. In the
light of the Gospel most modern formulations of the ideal of
freedom are therefore condemned. For most of those who pro-
fess to fight for freedom found their claim on a supposed rela-
tivity of truth. This "secularism" is the exact opposite of
Revelation.

In Christ Jesus all are free. This forms the gist of St. Paul's
message. There is neither slave nor slaveowner, for in Christ
all are one. Paul was not blind to facts. There were slaves and
there were masters to the eyes of men. Paul did not even inter-
fere with this unjust organization of society. When Onesimus,
the slave, took refuge near Paul, he was sent back to Philemon,
his master. The concept of liberty, according to which the
master is free to do what he likes with his slaves, is ignored.
The opposite idea, according to which the runaway slave tries
to start life on another basis, is also ignored. Neither is condemned, for the requirements of justice remain. Yet both are
brushed aside as irrelevant; redemption has made them outdated to a Christian. Whether a master or a slave in the

[1] John 8:32.
[2] 1 Cor. 1:23.

world, a Christian has been raised in baptism to a level where all is freedom.

Christian baptism creates an entirely new relation of man to the universe and to man. Freedom is no longer a subjective fulfillment of aspirations, the possibility of planning life for oneself according to one's desires and capabilities. Freedom becomes an objective state into which we are introduced: the state of those who have been delivered from the bondage of original sin. Yet Christian life is not lived in the clouds of a false mysticism. However free we may be on the supernatural level, we are nonetheless "in the world," subject to all the circumstances that block the free play of our likes and dislikes here below. The concrete problem of Christian freedom consists precisely in ascertaining what relationship exists, in one and the same man, between the liberty of those who have been redeemed and the bondage of those who are still in this world.

Theology has long been used to this dialectic between "free choice" and "freedom." Free choice (*liberum arbitrium* in the language of St. Augustine) is only, at best, preparatory for freedom (*libertas*). It can be the death of freedom, if we choose according to our evil inclinations. It can also mark our passage to spiritual adulthood, if we make our choice according to our natural desire for the vision of God. Viewed in this dynamic perspective, Christian freedom, granted in baptism, is only inchoate. It ensures the beginning of our pilgrimage toward the perfect freedom of heaven, when we shall be free enough to "judge the angels." Meanwhile, insofar as we live united with Christ, we are (or some of us are) enabled to understand St. Paul's statement that "a spiritual man judges all things; and he is judged by no one." Some saints attained to perfect spiritual freedom, the freedom of the children of God, yet never knew earthly conditions of life that would have given them the kind of elbow room that we associate with the "fulfillment of our opportunities."

In the sixteenth century the Reformation in general was well aware of this dual aspect of the problem of freedom. Luther himself saw it: "A Christian man is a perfectly free lord of all, subject to none. A Christian man is a perfectly dutiful servant of all, subject to all." [3] Spiritual freedom leads to service. Protestantism saw well enough the movement of the perfect Christian placing himself at the disposal of all. It did not see so clearly how imperfect Christians can pass from the freedom of choice that is theirs as men, to the spiritual liberty that must become theirs as Christians. Catholicism, which is more organic than Protestantism, has reached nearer to a solution.

This may be approached from the point of view of justice and love. It is a matter of justice to ensure that every human being will enjoy economic, social, cultural, and political conditions of life that may enable him freely to choose a way of life for himself. This is free choice. Since man is built for assuming responsibilities, this free choice is part of the human heritage. Its existence is a moral necessity for our human development. Yet its concrete forms are legitimately molded in the traditional social frameworks of our various societies. International justice does not consist in leveling these forms to an identical pattern. Its aim should rather be to respect each people's discovery and development of ways in which it finds the kind of freedom of choice that is congenial to itself. Social justice has to bring freedom of choice within the means of every citizen in our Western nations. When Christian love is not really mature, it does not always realize that unless we receive unusual graces we cannot reach the freedom of the children of God without a certain amount of human freedom of choice.

[3] *The Freedom of a Christian Man*, 1520.

Grace builds on the understructure of nature; baptism must be freely assented to. In the words of Cardinal Suhard, "Charity is good when it expresses love; it is evil when it hinders the practice of justice." Christian freedom is a lie if it does not attempt to develop conditions of life that ensure free choice to those who have not yet chosen. St. Thomas meant exactly this when he noticed that some human comfort is normally prerequisite to the practice of virtue. A certain freedom of choice is thus theologically necessary to Christian freedom. Justice, which guarantees it, is the ground in which love is born.

This is the basis of all Catholic social doctrine.

When freedom has apparently been reached, Christians are tempted to overlook the continued necessity of free choice. While he rose above the human problem of free choice in his time, Paul however did not overlook it. Philemon and Onesimus remain in the situation of master and of slave, yet both, since they are Christians, must behave so as to make Christian freedom effective in their actual situation. The details of this Paul left to them to discover when they would share the table of the Lord on equal terms. There is, however, a danger that this Pauline emphasis on the inner liberty of the Christian will be misconstrued as a denial of the necessity of free choice and exterior freedom.

That the last centuries of the Middle Ages fell into the temptation can hardly be questioned. The liberty of the children of God was thought to have become part of the cultural tradition of Christendom. Heresy was therefore repressed. Yet the possibility of heresy and of sin is a token that faith is free. "It is necessary that heresies come." [4] A passage from a recent address of Pope Pius XII may be quoted here with advantage. The Holy Father noted that the quarrels of the Church with

[4] 1 Cor. 11:19.

the State toward the end of the Middle Ages "have always tended to safeguard the liberty of religious convictions." He added: "Let it not be objected that the Church herself despises the personal convictions of those who do not think as she does. The Church did and does consider the voluntary rejection of the true faith to be a sin. When, from about 1200, this defection was made liable to penal repression both by civil and by religious authority, this was in order to avoid a breakup of the religious and ecclesiastical unity of the West. To non-Catholics the Church applies the principle embodied in the Code of Canon Law: 'Nobody may be forced to adopt the Catholic faith against his conscience.' She thinks that their convictions constitute a motive, though not the most important, of tolerance." [5]

Restraint of religious liberty was part of a civilization out of which it cannot be exported. It may be understood in the context of the times and in view of the importance of undividedness for the Christendom of that period. This, however, does not justify it in the absolute. For good order in society the free choice of citizens must have limits. These are set by natural morality or may be legitimately imposed by the State in view of the common good. Medieval legislators took their responsibilities according to the common good of Christendom as they saw it.

The situation of the last centuries has altered this common good. Pius XII noted it in the same document: "The Church does not hide the fact . . . that she considers the unity of the people in the true religion and unanimity of action between herself and the State as an ideal. But she knows that for a certain time now events have evolved in the opposite direction, toward a multiplicity of religious confessions and con-

[5] *Address to the 10th International Congress of Historical Sciences,* Sept. 7, 1955.

ceptions of life within the same national community, in which Catholics form a more or less important minority." In view of this situation, the tolerance of heresy within one nation has become essential to our common good.

A recurrent source of misunderstandings when dealing with our problem is that the modern world uses freedom as a rallying point while it covers many diverging ideas. Marxists claim that they have found liberty in the annihilation of free choice, thus aping the Christian concept of spiritual freedom. Americans are proud of their freedom of political choice and their social equality; yet in the name of their democratic way of life some businessmen would not be averse to establishing economic monopolies and dictatorships. The puzzle of colonialism is that colonialists and nationalists do not speak of the same kind of freedom. When they say that "we have done so much for them," the former state a fact that is usually true, but they overlook an important point: a good that is imposed and reluctantly received is no longer good. Free choice was a privilege in feudal society; it is a right to the eyes of nationalists with a modern education.

In the present conundrum the Church alone offers the unifying principle that is badly needed. In the first place she maintains that for those who have been assumed into the Mystical Body freedom in the truth transfigures the necessary or artificial limits of free choice. In the second she asserts with equal force that free choice is prerequisite to accepting the truth of the Gospel and thus reaching to the liberty of the children of God.

A common accusation says that the Catholic Church denies free choice to her members. Remarkably enough, the accusation always comes from non-Catholics. What happens is simple: what Catholics understand as "authority" is judged to be "tyranny" by others.

The concept of authority is widely misunderstood.

As traditionally interpreted by Catholic theology, *authority* is essentially connected with the idea of *authorship*. God has authority because He is the Author of the world. Christ has authority because He is the author of salvation. A man has authority because he is the father of his child. A State has authority because it strives to be the author of the common good within its territory. To say that someone is an authority on something is to recognize his total or partial authorship of it. Thus authority is accidental neither to its holder nor to its subjects; it is a constitutive relationship between them. Moral obligations follow from it when the persons involved are capable of moral choice.

To respect authority is therefore to respect a relation of origin. The Church has authority over her members because she is the mother of all the faithful; in her they were born to grace by baptism. As spiritual freedom coincides with grace, the conclusion is inescapable that in the Church authority and freedom are one. To say that the Church has authority is to recognize her as the channel of spiritual freedom.

On the contrary, an authority that would not be connected with some sort of authorship would be a tyranny. It is therefore normal that authority in the Church should be denounced as tyranny by those who do not know her as the vehicle of redemption. The anti-Catholic polemicists who condemn her "tyranny" are better witnesses than they know to the nature of her authority. For those who see the Church as the Bride of Christ there is, reversely, no problem of freedom in the Church; to be in the Church is freedom itself. This freedom grows with spiritual life. Hence the wisdom of St. Benedict when he wrote in his Rule: "Obedience to one another." For to obey a man is to make him our father in God, to entrust him with the common good of the Communion of the Saints. A society where every man would obey every other man would achieve perfect freedom and harmony. The society that comes nearest to this is the Church; the Supreme Pontiff himself is a "servant of servants."

Misuse of authority in the Church is always possible. It may even be frequent. This is understandable. For when we pass from the authority of the Church as the Mystical Body to the mediation of that authority by men, we enter a realm where ambiguity reigns. The only domain where authority in the Church cannot be misused is that of definitions of faith, protected as these are, in their formulations, by the infallible assistance of the Holy Spirit. Everything else is open to human slants and mistakes. In as far as they tend to promote or protect the common good of the Church, decisions with a bias also need obedience; their authority comes from their connection with the common good. The Holy Spirit guides the Church through them in spite of these occasional misusages due to human frailty. Compliance in this case expresses trust in the Spirit and His guidance. But "where the Spirit is, there is liberty." [6] Thus obedience to misuse of authority is an act of freedom. Only free men obey with a free judgment.

At bottom, the problem of adjusting obedience to authority and freedom is thus a false problem. This is true of authority in the Church. It is also true of every authority that is really legitimate, of every authority that follows on responsibility for a common good.

We may now perceive why movements that start with the ideal of liberty often end in tyranny. Instead of proceeding to a strict analysis of the nature and conditions of freedom, revolutionaries have made liberty into an idol. Because they are charged with emotionality, ideas of liberty, autonomy, independence unleash forces and passions. Because they are

[6] 2 Cor. 3:17.

bereft of their genuine intellectual contents they do not find in themselves sufficient power of self-control. At this point liberty becomes an idol. And every idol has tyrannical power. Hence it is that democracy often borders on dictatorship.

Is there a way out of a situation where liberty is constantly threatened by its own defenders? There is indeed one, and only one. It consists in having in our mind a conception of liberty that takes proper account of the distinction and connection between free choice and freedom. As long as Western secularists conceive liberty as a state of indifference to ends, where positive and negative choices have the same, or no, objective value, they lie open to two destructive consequences. In the first place it will be logical for them to oppose those for whom choice has a meaning, and to attack every dogmatic religion and every constructive philosophy of life. All do not go thus far, but at the expense of consistency. In the second place, one cannot see on what human ground their position is preferable to the "superior kind of freedom" willingly accepted by fascists or communists.

The way out of the dilemma of free choice and liberation consists in holding both of them in their proper places. Free choice is preliminary to man's access to freedom. The freedom of one man inspires him to work that others may have free choice too. Then voluntary obedience is the fruit of liberty. It protects the dignity of the human person by relating it to Him from whom all authorship derives.

five

The Church and
Totalitarian Society

As was hinted at in the foregoing chapter, the problem of freedom is closely connected in our day with the question of totalitarian régimes. Freedom may be negatively defined by opposition to its contrary, oppression. The most spectacular oppression experienced in this century has been, and still is, due to political creeds that claim the total allegiance of man. This is not to say that other varieties of tyranny have all been eliminated. Were it so, we could congratulate ourselves on a remarkable progress in the situation of man. This stage of evolution has unfortunately not yet been reached. All societies present examples of tyranny. Yet the tyranny of totalitarianism looms far above all others. It therefore calls for special treatment.

There is a great deal of confused thinking about totalitarianism. As soon as some liberties appear to be somewhat restricted, especially in connection with the rights of the individual conscience, we hear cries of "totalitarianism." Totalitarianism, however, does not simply mean a police state or an undemocratic system of government. Past ages have known absolute monarchies that were far from totalitarian, where a great amount of freedom was enjoyed. In the present decades the case of Spain may be mentioned. Its régime does limit the religious freedom of non-Catholics even as it restricts the political liberty of everybody. Yet it forces no ideology into the minds of its citizens. Freedom of thought is unquestioned. The difference between present-day Spain and totalitarian régimes lies precisely there: Spain has only a régime of authority. It imposes its governmental structure on the people without consulting them. A totalitarian government would not be satisfied with that. Totalitarianism attempts to force all into one ideology. The ideology may be Nazism, Fascism, or Lenin-Marxism. This makes little difference. Brainwashing is one technique used in this attempt. Other lands may invent other methods, more or less inhuman all. A common denominator remains: the totalitarian mind wants to transform all others to the image of itself.

The totalitarian state was born first in the totalitarian mind. This is no property of any one culture, theory, or creed. Two men may share the same opinion or faith. The one respects other convictions. The other cannot brook contradiction. In order not to be contradicted, he wants to assert his views into the minds of others. I am not competent to investigate the psychological origin of this turn of mind or to inquire what sort of social surroundings or educational method helps it to develop. Whatever its causes, the fact has to be registered.

The totalitarian mind can be characterized by its intolerance of other points of view. Contrary to what is often said, faith, in the Catholic sense of the term, is not intolerant. Intolerance may be the reaction of a faith which is not sure of itself. When faith is firmly held, solidly grounded in the Revelation of Christ, it does not need to be intolerant. It radiates. The respect of sincere persons goes to it spontaneously. It holds its ground without difficulty in the worst of conditions, among the most divergent opinions, in the midst of the most bewildering pluralism. A conviction that is too weak, however, can create a complex of inferiority that will seek compensation in intolerance. Thus the totalitarian tendency may happen to coexist with faith. Faith as such is not responsible for this. It is due to the imperfect transformation of intellectual convictions by a weak faith. In spite of what faith ought to be, a believer can become totalitarian. This example of the religious totalitarian mind is familiar enough. History has recorded the havoc it has worked. Catholics should be aware of the damage it can still cause among them. For this totalitarian manner of holding faith tends to spread panic around. If one thing lurks around the corner for the totalitarian mind, at least in our Western kind of society, it is failure. For views cannot be forced on others by way of authoritative assertion. Failure then breeds resentment. Resentment is highly contagious. It feeds on the disappointments that everyone sooner or later encounters.

Instances of the totalitarian mind at work may be borrowed from all sorts of fields. That philosophical opinions can be held with the fanaticism of the totalitarian mind is evident. The amazing development of Communism out of a dryly philosophical theory illustrates this. There are other instances of philosophical totalitarianism. The so-called democratic faith of our secularists is no less totalitarian for deriving from woolly theories about the Progress of Man (with capital initials). Political opinions often border on totalitarianism when they become systematic ideologies. Nationalism is a case in point today. Loyalty to a tribe, a national tradition, or a way of life may be a natural virtue. Yet when patriotism, love for my homeland, becomes intolerant of foreign patriotisms, it is totalitarian. This passage from a virtue to a vice can escape detection. Everyone would like to think that his nation is the best, that she has been chosen by God to guide others, that she is a beacon for those who look for a better way of life. This identification of a secular state of things with God's own program for mankind is a trap into which Christians can fall just like others, at the expense of some elements in the Catholicity of their faith. Democracies themselves are not infallibly protected from letting this overheated patriotism grow into a totalitarian conception of world politics. Self-defense from subversive convictions, necessary as it is, favors an attitude of suspicion and opposition that can get out of hand. Then every nonconformity looks suspect of treason. This milder form of totalitarianism can itself pave the way for its sharper forms.

That totalitarian governments have been possible is no mystery. Once the totalitarian mind is at work, a totalitarian régime, given a number of favorable conditions, follows logically. In several parts of the world the Church now lives under totalitarian régimes.

One point has to be readily admitted: any particular religion favors totalitarianism when it coincides with a political ideology. Whether religion should ever become a political ideology is highly questionable. Nevertheless the possibility of being one is patent. The Hebrew theocracy in some periods of the Old Testament could be called totalitarian if this appellation did not sound too modern for that. The Christian attempts at a theocracy, in the Catholic Middle Ages, in the Byzantine Empire, in Calvin's Geneva, or in some of the early American settlements, do all, by one aspect or another, bring to mind some features of the modern totalitarian state. The identification of religion with politics, however, belongs to a past stage in the history of political conceptions. It comes within the chapter of the philosophy of politics. Religion as such has little to do with it.

The totalitarian régimes that we face today are nonreligious.

In a sense, of course, they endeavor to replace the traditional religions by the cult of the State. They can thus be false religions in the full meaning of the term. There are enough elements in Marx's theories to form a pantheistic religion in which the historical process amounts to a self-revelation of God. It may well be that convinced Communist militants are thus inspired, in their eagerness to keep abreast of the historical process, by pseudoreligious motivations. However this may be, the fact that the Church is placed face to face with political totalitarianism raises several questions.

The threat that the Communist States constitute to their own citizens and to the rest of the world is likely to make Catholics oblivious of a basic doctrine: the State's authority derives from God. This was the evident teaching of the New Testament and of the Church Fathers in respect to the persecuting Roman emperors. Whatever the origin of the State, it is entitled to the compliance of its citizens insofar as its decisions do not run counter to natural law and to Catholic faith. That the State was legitimate in its coming to power is a debatable matter. Whether its constitution is good or ought to be improved is equally questionable. This, however, is not the point. As soon as a given State is the only agency in a position to ensure the common temporal good of a nation, it has authority in the theological sense of the term. This concept of authority was explained in the previous chapter. It applies equally well to a democracy and to a dictatorship, to a republic and to a monarchy. In the practical application of this concept, therefore, the Church is not concerned with the *rights* of this or that family, of one party or another, to hold and organize the government. She is interested in knowing what is, *in fact,* the present form of the State. As a consequence of this traditional conception of the *de facto* authority of the State, Catholics living in the self-styled popular democracies of the present time are, to a certain extent, caught in a dilemma. Their régime can claim their loyalty in political matters, that is, in matters that concern the common good of their country. Yet it wages a more or less open, but always relentless, war on the Church and her faith, which are also entitled to their loyalty. Neither of those facts should eclipse the other. Neither of these allegiances should be destroyed by the other. In final analysis they form one loyalty only: to the Church and her traditional interpretation of civic authority.

Christians who are caught on the horns of this dilemma need a great deal of theological discernment. They have to sort out in the government's acts what is and what is not in keeping with the Christian conscience. The cunning of the government itself and the unavoidable play of personal preferences are bound to bring about a certain hesitancy in many cases. This in turn can lead to Catholics reaching diverse decisions in particular matters. The occasional reports about Catholics in opposition and so-called "progressives" in Poland or elsewhere are well in harmony with this analysis of the situation. In the absence of adequate information, it is hardly possible from afar to distribute blame or praise with justice. Reflection on this, however, shows as clear as day that the Catholic laity of the twentieth century has to be singularly well formed in religious questions to be able to stand its ground when that sort of tribulation befalls it. What has happened in one part of the world can also take place in another. No nation or continent is immune to this.

I am fully aware that for some trends in American society Christianity is more or less identified with a democratic way of life. Much as democracy is to be appreciated, one must maintain that the Catholic Church as such cannot be involved in an absolute endorsement of democratic society. What matters, to the eyes of the Catholic tradition, is that government, whatever its form and the immediate origin of its authority, be guided by the twin concepts of the temporal good of its citizens and of the universal good of world society. The pluralistic structure of modern life, both on the national and on the international level, must be taken into account when this common good is defined in a concrete instance.

In a number of public pronouncements in recent years Pope Pius XII applied these principles to the main problems of the postwar world. These documents constitute important chapters in a possible synthesis of Catholic thought in matters of international and national policy today. The late Pope's Christmas messages explicitly dealt with the present world crisis. In 1951 the Church's contribution to peace was analyzed. In 1952 political dilemmas were traced back to a basic lack of concern for the human person. In 1953 the technological society, both in its Communist and in its capitalistic forms, was criticized as essentially inhuman. In 1954 conditions for a change in international relations and a lessening of tensions were laid down. In 1955 the Pope warned against the dangers inherent in a predominantly industrial age. In 1956 he described the contradictions of our time in the light of Christian realism. In 1957 the disharmony of man, who is materially more successful and spiritually more frustrated than formerly, was traced back to materialistic philosophies. Christ was shown to be the focal point of any effective system of order and harmony.

Outside of these major messages Pius XII made many addresses on similar topics. He encouraged the formation of a system of punitive laws in international relations (October 3, 1953). He insisted on the necessity and conditions of the tolerance of religious pluralism in order to promote peace among nations (December 6, 1953). He treated of the relations between Church and State in a historical perspective

(September 7, 1955). He indicated on what basis armed conflicts should be prevented (October 13, 1955). To such a promotion of the human person in and through national and international politics the Church is undoubtedly committed. She is not thereby bound to support any particular form of government.

Democracy in general or any one of its particular varieties does not constitute the earthly form of the kingdom of God. The Church is therefore not pledged to democracy as a system of political administration. Democracy she encourages as the aim to which political efforts should tend. Yet she remains indifferent to the form of government actually in use in the various countries of the world. All régimes she judges on their acts.[1] This brings about a conflict with all political régimes as soon as they turn totalitarian. For, as we have said, the totalitarian State tries to eradicate ideologies that are not its own. From its seat of power over the minds of its citizens, it sees Catholic life, from the outside, as nourished by what seems to be a competing philosophy. This conflict may remain virtual as long as the totalitarian State has not decided on the strategy of its attack on the Church. It comes into the open once faith has been hindered in some of its legitimate manifestations or implications. This happens also whenever a government that is structurally democratic adopts totalitarian views in religious matters. This is why a latent disagreement opposes the Church and some political parties or tendencies in Western countries concerning problems of education. Western secularists who want to ensure the "Progress" of mankind through purely secular education sooner or later fight the Church. In so doing they are more consistent than they know

[1] This indifference justifies the separation of Church and State from the Church's point of view. It also shows that no misbehavior on the part of the State can escape the judgment of the Church.

and than we often judge them: the totalitarian mind, here as in other matters, cannot stand pluralism. Just like the totalitarian Communist, the totalitarian secularist wishes to destroy the Church. She is the archenemy of the totalitarian mind.

At this point in our survey of the totalitarian trends of our times, it comes to mind that the preceding statement on the Church's being the foe of totalitarianism is exactly opposite to what a certain literature in America has been saying for years. To keep ourselves to relatively recent publications, the productions of Paul Blanshard are now notorious. There is no doubt, if we are to believe Paul Blanshard and others, that the most totalitarian institution on earth is the Roman Catholic Church. Catholic totalitarianism, we are told, prepares its Nazi or Marxist substitutes by wooing the preoccupations of Catholics away from democracy; it fights an underground war on the American way of life and thus undermines the resistance of the United States to Communist imperialism. One sees well enough the core of Blanshard's arguments: the Church claims the total spiritual allegiance of her members; by thus depriving them of a man's right to his private judgment (as seen by Blanshard) she encourages a blind obedience which is likely to accept totalitarian politics.

Paul Blanshard is naturally very happy when his views find an apparent justification in the practical intolerance of some Catholics. By a process that comes easily to men who do not share the Catholic understanding of the Church, the faults of some of her members are unduly attributed to the whole Institution. The narrowness of some moralists and the polemics in which a few theologians waste their time fill him with joy. All this, for Paul Blanshard, points, not to the stupidity of particular persons (Baptism, according to Catholic theology, does not confer intelligence on those who have none), but to the essence of the Church. Actually, the Church does not condone, though she may forgive, the moral failure, the intellectual shortcomings, or the deplorable public relations for which her members may be responsible. In the Church as elsewhere, the faithful often fall short of the ideal that has been proposed to them. This happens in spite of the Church. Yet it causes more joy to her foes than it disturbs her. In her wisdom she knows men as sinners and fools all. Their weaknesses matter indeed a great deal, yet on a superficial plane only. The Church's life is not there. It is in the experience of the liturgy, in the awareness of Christ's presence, in the certainty of the Spirit's guidance. This mystery of the Church lies beyond human frailties.

Needless to say, the authentic nature of the Church escapes Paul Blanshard's experience and understanding. I am therefore not concerned with the details of his contentions. His views do not stand or fall by their accuracy.[2] Whatever their worth, his picture of the Church is radically biased from the start because Paul Blanshard does not know what he is talking about. How could an out-and-out secularist understand the Church, that admirable encounter of God and man in the Body of Christ? There are, admittedly, non-Catholic religious figures who also indulge in attacks on the "totalitarianism of the Roman Church" (as they say). This only shows that such polemicists, however religious they may be as their religion goes, do not grasp the meaning of the Catholic Church any better than Paul Blanshard.

There still remains a problem here. For even when he fails to see what the Church means to a Catholic conscience, an

---

[2] It is my confirmed impression that Catholic answers to Blanshard have, in general, paid too much attention to the details of his accusations. These may all be disproved one by one, and his general thesis remains untouched. What matters is the principle of Blanshard's interpretation of the facts that he digs out. There lies what is to his mind the strength, and to mine, the abysmal hollowness of his assertions.

intelligent outsider should be able to be fair to her. Many are. I do not speak here of those who judge her to be totalitarian just because they believe the misrepresentations that they have read or heard of her doctrine and her activities. These good people should be excused, just like ignorant Catholics who are unfair to positions they know little about. The point here is that men can have studied the Church, up to a point, as best they could. Yet their judgment has utterly missed what she means. My concern goes to those who sincerely believe that they ought to perpetuate or revamp these misrepresentations and, by doing so, misrepresent her still more. This is another case where the totalitarian mind is at work. The totalitarian mind condemns what it does not understand. Elements that are out of tune with its own system have to be done away with. They are the enemy. This is ironical enough, but far from unusual: the totalitarian mind blames totalitarianism on others in order to fight them. This has been common in the tactics of all anti-Catholics, either political or religious.

The frequent denunciations of the Church as a totalitarian system of thought point once more to what constitutes a motive of this book: the need for an articulate, well formed, competent Catholic laity. Only the existence of such a body of lay Catholics can give the lie to those who see the Church as the great obstacle in the way of a properly developed manhood. In the secularistic frame of mind of today, this factual argument alone can be efficacious. We can go on repeating, as I have myself done, that secularism misses the point. As long as the élite of the Catholic laity is not developed in proportion to its religious and other responsibilities, our theological precisions can only meet a shrug of the shoulders.

six

Conversion to the Church

When Saul was stricken on the way to Damascus he saw the Lord Jesus. Rising from the ground he was disposed to give himself to the Master he had persecuted hitherto. Yet he was blind. The Lord Who had conquered his heart did not tell him what to do. He did not wish to make Saul into one of those who seek for miracles in order to believe. The vision blinded Saul not only to the outward scenery but also to the meaning of life ahead of him. "For three days he was without sight, and neither ate nor drank." Like the three days of Jonas in the fish, like the three days of Jesus in the underworld, these three sightless days are symbolic of the death that preludes resurrection. Saul had died with Jesus to his former self. To what new existence was he about to rise?

Light dawned upon Saul when, through Ananias the prophet, he was received in the fellowship of the Church: "Brother Saul, the Lord Jesus who appeared to you on the road by which you came, has sent me that you may regain your sight and be filled with the Holy Ghost." The Church is sent to those to whom the Lord has revealed Himself. And the outcome is rising to new life: "Immediately something like scales fell from his eyes and he regained his sight. Then he rose and was baptized." [1]

The conversion of St. Paul throws light on the structure of conversion.

Conversion is an event in two moments. A first stage in the total process consists in acknowledging, in the words of Paul, that "Jesus is Lord, to the glory of God the Father." [2] Paul went through it on the way to Damascus, when Jesus appeared to him. In the ideal type of conversion, from paganism to Catholicism, this stage is achieved when we are convinced that all honor and obedience are due to Christ Who is the Lord Incarnate, God made man, the center of attraction and the poise of all things visible and invisible. The way we reason that out, if we ever do so, does not matter; and any sort of event may have lit the spark that brought us light. When, after our discovery of Christ, we explain what took place, we project back into the past a whole set of subsequent impressions that were not there originally. The psychological process is indeed difficult to assess, and conversion stories are often misleading.

Theologically faith results from two elements: an acquaintance with the Person of Christ (through reading or hearing about Him) and a divine intervention, called the "light of faith," whereby our soul is illumined to such a point that we stake our life on the truth of Christ.

At this first moment of conversion, the "light of faith," received in an acquiescing heart, shows unmistakably that what has been heard of the Lordship of Christ is the truth: He is for us the Way, the Truth and the Life. But everything else remains in the dark. Like Paul we are still blinded; we have to grope our way to Damascus. Faith is a night.

In the second moment of his conversion, Paul discovered

[1] Acts 9:17–19.
[2] Philippians 2:11.

the Church. The Church at the same time discovered him. Ananias was sent by Christ and found that Saul the persecutor was disposed to serve the Lord. The function of the Church at this stage of the process of conversion is only that: to know to whom Christ has revealed Himself and to open her fellowship to them. The Church is then discovered as the prophetic and institutional community wherein Christ lives till the end of the world. In her the "convert" discerns the presence of Christ. His own commitment to Christ illumines his judgment on the Church and he sees her as a work of God. The "light of faith" connotes God's works. Ananias and Saul know each other as brothers in Christ. The Church and the "convert" mutually acknowledge the presence of the Lord in themselves.

The difference between these two moments in conversion is distinctly marked in the Creed. We say *Credo in Deum* but *Credo Ecclesiam.*[3] The omission of *in* is significant. We believe *in* God but not *in* His works, of which the Church is one. We believe only that His works are and that they are good.

The Church's role in conversion is therefore most humble. She may not substitute herself for God. She may not induce people to believe *in* her, to think that she replaces Christ. Her mission is rather to preach the Gospel in such a way that all have a chance to understand it (first moment of conversion). Then she has to be discovered by and to discover those who now believe in Christ (second moment). The first step amounts to developing her missionary life. The second comes to witnessing to the presence of Christ within her so that all who believe in Him may also see that the Church is Christ's, and receiving in her fellowship those who have discovered her.

[3] A priest having read these lines expressed doubts as to the latinity of *Credo Ecclesiam.* The point could be solved by consulting a Latin grammar. I should, however, like to refer the matter to the Catechism of the Council of Trent: *Ecclesiam credere oportet, et non in Ecclesiam* (Part I, ch. 23)—"We must believe the Church, not in the Church."

Preaching her Lord, being faithful to Him, baptizing into herself: the Church has no other part to play.

In the light of these remarks, the present situation seems to be dominated by obvious anomalies.

The two moments of conversion are often so dissociated that in some cases no recognition of the Church ever takes place. This raises no problem in the theology of faith, for if "three days" can separate the two moments of conversion, there is no reason why they could not be indefinitely prolonged. The problem rather concerns the theology of the Church: How is it that the mutual encounter between the "convert" and the Church, in which each recognizes the other, does not come off?

Presumably, the Church has not been met under such an aspect that the "light of faith" could illumine her connection with Christ. Today's non-Catholic Christians stand in that paradoxical situation where Saul was before meeting Ananias. Knowing the externals of the Church, they cannot relate them to their interior meaning and so they must refuse the fellowship offered by the Church to all who believe in Christ.

The attitude of Catholics toward other Christians must, accordingly, be altogether different from their approach to unbelievers. The lazy habit of calling "Protestants" people who belong to no definite religion has the disastrous result that one becomes unable to deal with the issue of divided Christendom. Leaving aside the problem of unbelievers, which calls for a missionary approach adapted to the paganism of our modern cities and countries, let us now concentrate on the conversion of non-Catholic Christians.

That there are genuine Christians who deny the Church is made possible by the necessary ambiguity affecting all realities that participate in the events of history. The faults and failures of the men who are in the Church, their twofold engagement in faith and in secular activities, their occasional insincerity, throw shadows on the garments of the Church. Because of them she is more or less hidden behind a haze of equivocation. This is unavoidable as long as the members of the Church remain sinners, which they are bound to remain. It follows upon the nature of history, whereby the kingdom of God is prepared through men who are unworthy of that kingdom. Yet to some extent it may be reduced.

Connected with this point, the present situation exhibits a second, hardly avoidable, anomaly. Some are members of the Church who have never known Christ. The truths of faith have been accepted as theoretical propositions unrelated to their existence; or they are a matter of habit. Catholicism has then become a way of life with social connotations that make its profession desirable. The Church as an institution is taken for granted but the Church as a continuous prophecy of God is ignored.

This is clearly the more basic anomaly. Because of it the ambiguity projected by history upon the outward aspect of the Church creates an estrangement between their faith and their knowledge of the Church in the conscience of separated Christians.

We can now determine the exact scope of our duties concerning the conversion of these Christians to the fullness of Revelation.

Let us not treat them as though they were non-Christians. It is entirely out of focus to concentrate on proselytism, to try to induce our Protestant acquaintances into entering a Church unawares, to entangle them in convert drives or bring them over to convert classes. So-called techniques for convert making are of no avail where believing Christians are concerned: their need is not for apologetical arguments, but for the testimony of a life utterly given to Christ. The modern man does not believe in logic. But he is sensitive to experience and personal witness. What he needs to see is that the Church makes for better Christianity. This is why Pope Adrian VI in 1522 ascribed the rupture of Christian unity to the evil hearts of Catholics: "You must say," he enjoined his legate Chieregati, "that we freely acknowledge that God permitted this persecution of the Church to take place on account of the sins of men, especially of priests and prelates." [4]

In other words, the true work for the reunion of separated Christians does not lie in arguing their convictions away, but in purifying ourselves, that they may see the Church in a better light. Non-Catholic Christians will find their way back to Mother Church when, both individually and all together, Catholics witness through their life to the fact that they belong to the Church of the Creed: not only *unam* and *apostolicam,* but moreover *sanctam* and *catholicam.*

Adulthood may be measured by readiness to face facts. Now two facts clamor for a hearing. In the first place, although the number of Catholics has steadily grown in the last years, their proportion in world population has diminished at a regular pace. Absolute statistics score higher and higher figures; yet comparison would seem to show that we are becoming a less and less important minority. In the second place, non-Catholic Christians are not coming over. What Dom Chapman, of Downside Abbey, remarked in 1937 is still valid: "We lose as many people at the bottom of the scale as we gain at the top, and our total growth does not compare with the growth of population. At the present rate one cannot say that England is being converted to Roman Catholicism." With some local gains which are absorbed in the general stalemate, this gives the picture all the world over as regards separated Christians. And to imagine, as some apparently do, that Russia will be-

[4] *Instructio data Francisco Chieregato,* in J. Le Plat, *Monumentorum . . . collectio,* Vol. 2, p. 147.

come Catholic all of a sudden as soon as she is out of her present régime is a piece of wishful thinking that nothing can possibly substantiate.

Nor are we doing anything of importance than can alter the situation. As far as the reunion of Christendom is concerned, the method which lumps together Christians and unbelievers forms the backbone of most approaches to the problem. Yet it is called for neither by the theological structure of conversion nor by the psychological make-up of separated Christians. What we want is quite another thing: a witness by Catholics, in every activity where they can possibly share, that the Church is the home divinely prepared for mankind. Witnessing does not consist in staking claims but in sharing an experience. It must be present wherever men work, not only in ordinary walks of life, but in all fields of technical research and disinterested scholarship.

No better guide for this may be found than Pius XII, who devoted a sizable part of his many addresses to a friendly and up-to-date appraisal of the contribution of science and scholarship to a more thorough knowledge of the world, of man, and of God. These three elements—the world, man, and God— are dovetailed in the plan of salvation centered upon the Incarnation. Real Christian witness must be a tribute to the greatness of all three. It must make fuel of all. To underrate the first two in a desire to extol the third is a treason. When Catholic thought has thus recovered the leadership of sciences, arts, and cultures, those who have met Christ will have a chance to recognize His Church: whose holiness will be reflected in the commitment of her members; whose Catholicity will be manifested through her presence in all the fields where the spirit of man is at work.

Besides this properly intellectual apostolate, which ought to cover theology and secular arts and sciences, there is needed most of all a reawakening of Catholics to a life of common worship. The brotherhood of men means nothing when it is not grounded in the fatherhood of their Creator. It will not come about by appealing to good will or common sense or the fear of an aggressive atheism; it will follow upon a closer realization of our divine adoption in Christ. However holy we may be in our lives, we do not witness to Our Lord as we should as long as we do not appear collectively consecrated to Him. The first Christians were called "the saints," not because of their virtues, which were then as dubious as they still are, but because of their common partnership in the Eucharistic "holy things"—the Body and Blood of the Lord sacramentally received in the sacred meal of the Christian family.

When our Masses are something better than a juxtaposition of a private service at the altar and private devotions in the benches; when our assistance at church is something else than a crowd where each stands unconnected with his neighbor; when our liturgy is truly the visible continuous rebirth of our fellowship in the Saviour, then Christians outside the Church will have a chance to see her as the fulfillment of the promise, "Blessed are ye poor, for yours is the kingdom of God." [5] The poor in the biblical sense are those who trust in nothing but the Lord from Whom they now receive the heavenly food of the sacraments, as their ancestors received manna in the wilderness. And the kingdom of God is the "dwelling of God with men," [6] the city which has "no temple, for its Temple is the Lord God Almighty and the Lamb." [7] It is the New Jerusalem which is already inchoate in the Church and wherein we participate through the liturgy.

A spiritual renewal that shows forth in the intellectual apos-

[5] Luke 6:20.
[6] Roman liturgy.
[7] Apoc. 21:22.

tolate and the liturgical movement is for Catholics the only way of contributing to the "conversion" of other Christians.

Then the Church, having known her children all along, will receive them in.

Ananias will no longer distrust Saul, and Saul will be strengthened through Ananias.

seven

The Reintegration
of Non-Catholics

Whether we like it or not, we live in one society with men who do not share our faith or share it only in part. From the standpoint of practical politics, this raises a problem: how best to organize a pluralistic society. The modern democratic State respects the consciences of all citizens and accordingly abstains from intervention in the domain of religious convictions. As a matter of fact the United States has developed a system which has, on the whole, worked out satisfactorily, with no claim to perfection.

From the point of view of Catholic theology, discussions concerning Church and State among Catholic writers of this country seem to have established one point. The neutral attitude adopted by the Constitution toward organized religion is entirely in keeping with the requirements of Catholic doctrine. The few voices who still favor the opposite view lead a rear-guard action for an opinion that is fast disappearing. At times they read the American situation in the light of a conception of the State which may have been valid in the Middle Ages but which does not fit the empirical realities of our time and place.

My purpose is not, however, to go over the question of Church and State. The coexistence of Catholics with other Christians posits other problems also. A certain tendency has been prone to reduce the duty of Catholics toward their separated brethren to a mere duty of conversion. This is an over-simplification of the issue. A frequent form of escapism refuses to face a problem by first suppressing the data. As a result, the modern scene is not viewed as it actually is. This sort of escapism has been at work in the present field of the behavior of Catholics toward their separated brethren. In this matter it tends to overlook the proper requirements of what is now called, in a somewhat unfortunate phrase, Catholic "ecumenism."

The last thirty years have witnessed the rise of this movement in a number of countries. With the liturgical movement and the theological awakening of our day, this powerfully contributes to the Catholic revival that we are experiencing. Its proper contribution is to further, from the point of view of Catholic doctrine and life, the quest after unity which is nowadays widely favored outside the Roman Catholic Church. If we are interested in the canonical aspects of the movement, its official charter so far is an instruction from the Holy Office published in 1949, in which Bishops in relevant areas are urged to be actively concerned in that work.

The task of Catholics here is on two levels. There is, first, the field of scholarly research and writing. It is open to specialists of theology and of Church history. We shall not deal with this at length. It will be more to the point to draw attention to an aspect in which all can and should take part: the wide field of prayer for Christian unity and for the sanctification of all according to the will of God.

The attitude which marks Catholic "ecumenism" may be distinguished from a mainly polemical or even apologetical method. A polemical method, instead of arguing in a detached manner, makes fuel of personal arguments. Most of the first adversaries of Luther were not unwilling to have recourse to abuse. They may be excused. Luther did not spare them either. Yet this attitude does considerable harm. At the present time, fortunately, relations between Catholics and non-Catholics are usually more gentlemanly. This is all for the better.

An apologetical method obtained during most of the centuries that have elapsed since the break-up of Christendom into rival sections. Sound it certainly was. Yet it cannot be said to have been efficient. For it leveled philosophical arguments at religious positions. In order to be convincing, a rational argument has to be logical. To be logical it must use philosophical categories, however embryonic the underlying philosophy may be. This creates a vicious circle when we discuss Protestantism. The philosophical basis of Catholic apologetics is indeed theoretically adequate as far as liberal Protestantism is concerned. For liberal Protestantism also established its abode on philosophical ground. As regards the questions raised by classical Protestantism, however, and, still more, by Eastern Orthodoxy, this apologetics is beyond its depth. The positions of the Orthodox Churches and those of Protestantism in its origin are not philosophical but religious. They are connected with a Christian experience that may be biased, but is nonetheless to be accounted for. Eastern Orthodoxy is itself steeped in Patristic traditional thought. Now a philosophy cannot hold the field against a theology. If it could, Christianity would be just another rationalistic system.

That apologetical attitude may still be met with in outmoded manuals. It tends to consider all heterodox doctrines as, first, opinions to be attacked. They may have to be attacked eventually. Before that, however, they have to be understood. This is why the best works that Catholics have recently contributed to the modern search after unity are highly constructive essays. They are grounded in the renewal of Patristic studies which has been so remarkable in this first half-century. They take account of the exigencies of a historical method of research. They thus try to establish a basis for future agreements rather than directly to eradicate past and present disagreements.

This change of focus ought not to be restricted to scholars. It should be brought down also to the level of the people at large. This is where all are called on to enter the largely unchartered realm of prayer for Christian unity. Admittedly, leaflets or posters occasionally advocate prayer for Christian unity. In some areas this is even organized on a wide scale, especially during the "Chair of Unity Octave" (January 18–25). Pioneers are always trying to hit on new and better ways of driving the idea home. Yet it seems, in the main, that the conditions for an adequate prayer for Christian unity are not only unfulfilled, but even hardly suspected. Only by praying much do we reach deep enough into ourselves to pray in the right way. Lip service to Christian unity is easy. It is infinitely more demanding to orient our life in the way of accepted suffering which alone gives depth to prayer. The progressive intimacy with God which Christians experience when they pray follows a pattern of its own when it is approached from the standpoint of prayer for Christian unity.

I should like to draw attention briefly to some aspects of this pattern. They are prerequisites to the fulfillment of prayer for Christian unity. We do pray. Yet as long as that prayer is not lived at the deepest level of personality, an answer cannot be expected. "The Word of God is more piercing than a two-edged sword . . . and reaches unto the division of the soul and the spirit." [1] A word of God is embodied in the "priestly

[1] Heb. 4:12.

prayer" of Christ for unity: it has to be read in such a way that it goes down to the extreme depth of the soul.

If we analyze the underlying assumptions of a Catholic ecumenical attitude, we find that now more than ever before in history we are becoming aware on a large scale of the dilemma which is posited to the Christian conscience.

Ever since the growing apart of the Eastern and the Western sections of the medieval Church, the seeds of a dilemma have been sown. They sprouted into the open with the Reformation and the Counter Reformation. What had been, and ever remains, in our faith, the unchallenged Catholic doctrine on the essential unity of the Church, ran foul of a fact: Christian disunion. Christian persecution, when each side proceeded to exterminate the other in the name of their common Lord, brought this to a head. In metaphysical terms, there has been since the sixteenth century a tension between the undivided essence of the Catholic Church and the circumstances of her temporal existence. In theological terms, the picture that we draw of the Church in what medieval theologians called our "morning knowledge" does not easily fit what our "evening knowledge" sees of her. Our "morning knowledge" (or knowledge in the Word of God) shows her as the one spotless Bride of Christ. Our "evening knowledge" (or knowledge through the senses) knows that the Church has been, and to a certain extent still is, a stone of scandal for many of our separated brethren. There is no question of denying what faith knows on account of what eyes see. There is no possibility either of hiding what we see behind what we believe. Catholic ecumenism thinks that there is a way out of the dilemma. This way was not truly opened, though it may have been indicated, by the former attitude in apologetics. It lies (and this holds good for all Christians) in faithfulness to the Holy Spirit who dwells in us. For the ultimate cause of Christian disunion is rooted in the heart. Our heart also is one in Christ. Yet it is pulled asunder by the strength of unholy thoughts and desires. But each of the faithful is an epitome of the whole Church. He is responsible for the plight of the Church. "You are the Body of Christ and its members, each for his own part." [2]

This interconnection of the whole and the parts cannot be questioned. The only thing, then, is to apply to prayer for the unity of the Church and for the reconciliation of Christians what the experience of the saints has shown to be required by the purification of prayer in general.

"The means through which the soul reaches to divine union is made neither of thought nor of pleasure, of feeling or of attempts to imagine God . . . : it is made of pureness and love, that is to say, it is the foregoing and renouncing of all things for God's sake." [3] St. John of the Cross said this of the soul in particular. It may be applied to her as responsible for the Church. The way to Christian reconciliation does not run through complacency in our own security. It ignores sentimental enthusiasm or artificial schemes and blueprints. It does not even wind its way over the sole fields of intellectual research and discussion. All this may have its use. The last item is certainly indispensable. It may at times provide good ground for hope. Yet there is a requirement of unity which is not met by mere study. The way to the reconciliation of non-Catholics is a footpath that slowly crosses over the desert of spiritual renouncement in the night of pure faith. If and when the day of reunion finally dawns, it will not be due firstly to the efforts of apostles or to the attempts of leaders to bridge abysses of separations. It will be the work of thousands of humble souls who, throughout the Christian world, will have prayed and suffered in their longing after a reunion that they

[2] Cor. 12:27.
[3] *The Ascent of Mount Carmel,* bk. II, ch. 4.

could not themselves see. The key that will open the gate leading all Christians in the one fold will be forged in sacrifice.
The first sacrifice to be made is the purification of faith.
The Church is a spiritual reality whose life is no other than
the life of the Incarnate Lord Himself. As such she exclusively
depends on the will of Christ. She is one as He is one. The one
and only Church is mediated through the men and women
who are her members on earth. This is the institutional aspect
of the Church militant. In its structural elements, the Institution is inseparable from the Mystical Body of Christ, of which
it is the sacramental expression on earth. Faith adheres to it
as to Christ Himself. But a landslide easily takes place. One
then transfers to the essence of the Church, and thereby to
Christ, secondary elements that appear and disappear, in fact,
as circumstances require. To take an example of this process.
The Catholic faith holds that the See of St. Peter in Rome
shall always be the center of the Church as Institution. There
shall be no reunited Christendom as long as this traditional
doctrine is not recognized by separated Christians. Many,
however, wittingly or no, go much further. As defined by the
Councils, the Church is "Roman" in her visible head; but she
is not "Latin." Latin Christendom is only, next to an Eastern
Christianity, a section of the Church. Yet one is tempted to
take it for granted that the present discipline of the Latin
Church, with its customs, its rites, its ethos, and its canonical
system, is also part and parcel of the necessary framework of
unity. If we look at it closely, no doubt remains that this Latin
Christianity, venerable as it is, is the outcome of the cultural
development of western Europe. As culture changes, the cor-
responding religious habits evolve also. This is true of canonical discipline as it is of liturgical rites. Faith indeed identifies
the Catholic Church with the Mystical Body of Christ. Hope
looks forward to a day when interior inherence in the Body

of Christ will always coincide with exterior allegiance to the Catholic Church. Neither faith nor hope, however, teaches what rites or what discipline will prevail in the Church at that time, be it near or far. To imagine that the reunion of separated Christians will take such or such a form is a mirage, no matter what particular form may be envisaged or wished. To entertain this kind of thinking is to admit an unwarranted accretion to the purity of faith. It is, accordingly, an obstacle thrown in the way to reintegration. Before there can be any serious thought of being all visibly joined, Christians have to purify their thinking. This means clinging to the only rock of the faith. It entails a suffering. For faith is a night. It refuses to throw artificial lights on the Revelation entrusted to the Church.

Hope needs also a serious purification. By definition hope bears on the help that God grants us, without which no man would reach salvation. Hope in the grace of Christian reunion is pure if one accepts being in the dark as to the precise conditions that will make reunion possible. Christians are agreed in their common faith in the Incarnate Lord (since this is the definition of Christianity). History has built a wall in the midst of them. And history is in the hands of God. Protestants maintain that separations, and the Reformation in particular, are providential events. Through these, as they assume, a message came from God. God's positive will upon His Church would be expressed through Protestantism in spite of the separations of Christians. Catholics, on the contrary, believe, in continuity with the pre-Reformation Church, that Christ's gift of unity to His disciples knows no repentance. The divisions of Christians are slants due to human frailty, lack of proportion, and sin. All agree, in any case, that the course of history cannot be reversed. One cannot simply return to unity as though five centuries could be stricken off the record. Unity is given in the Catholic Church; and those who are separated can come forward to her. But ultimate reconciliation transcends man's efforts. In the doctrine of the great Catholic mystics, hope becomes purer when we forego particular forms, ideas, programs, projects, thoughts, desires, and so forth, except those of God's own choosing. Neither faith nor hope makes us privy to what will happen tomorrow. The grace that God holds in store for the Church is ever expected and never previewed. Hearts must be ready to receive it whatever it is. We must therefore abstain from pinning our hope to what is not God Himself. The following maxim of St. John of the Cross can then be applied to those who hope for the reunion of separated Christians: "God has such high regard for the hope of a soul who looks always to Him and never to any other object whatsoever, that it may be said of that soul: she receives all that she hopes for." [4]

Hope in Christian union will get its first, perhaps its only, chance to be fulfilled when we pray for the conversion of non-Catholics as and when God wills it. This does not mean giving up faith or even theology. Far from it. It only entails an acknowledgment that faith expresses only partial truths about what God is and God wants.[5] The secret ways to a reintegrated Christendom may be hidden in what has not been revealed. Beyond what we know through Scripture, beyond what tradition teaches, there stretches the boundless night of what has not been perceived. A hope that is untainted by self-pride is

---

[4] *Maxims:* on hope.

[5] Readers who are superficially acquainted with Thomism may be surprised at this statement. Yet St. Thomas makes it clear that the Revelation to the angels was "much more excellent" than that made to the prophets and the apostles (v.gr., *S.T.*, I, q.57, a.5, ad 3). But Christian doctrine is founded on the "Revelation made to the apostles and the prophets" (*S.T.*, I, q.1, a.8, ad 2). To us, therefore, God has not revealed Himself as fully as He might have done.

content to be in the dark as to the means and methods. It adores the aim in the unknown designs of God: the gathering of Christians from all communions around the See of Peter, all sharing the same faith imparted to the Apostles and transmitted through the Roman Catholic Church.

The purification of Christian love is the most difficult. It implies not only altering personal views and making them subservient to the darkness of faith, but also changing our behavior. This goes very far. If I love my brother I also respect his convictions. I may not share them. I may have to reject them in conscience, in the name of my faith or of the faith of the Church. And yet, while condemning them, I respect them independently of their truth or of their error, in as far as they are my brother's. Everything that engages the love of men, to which men dedicate their lives, is worth respecting. Clearly, suspension of judgment requires a real sacrifice. Yet this is in many cases the only Christian behavior. By loving somebody who does not share our convictions, we do not thereby cease to believe and to let him know what our faith is. But we do not question the sincerity of his motives. In order to commune with the man himself, we learn to see things from the viewpoint that prevails in his mind. This does not lead us to share his point of view, if it is out of focus. It leads us to respect it.

There are objections. "To love man, but to hate error." From a metaphysical point of view, it seems hard to understand how error can be an object of hatred. For we cannot hate what is not. An error is a lack of truth—that is, a lack of being. It can be healed or rectified, or whatever we may call it. But it cannot be hated. Furthermore, one should always remember, though one usually forgets, that although truth is objective, adhesion to truth is a subjective action. Everyone proceeds to it according to his lights. Responsibility cannot be judged by

reference to absolute standards. The lights that we have enjoyed must be assessed first. This is true of man's acceptance
of Revelation as it is of human judgments. When a Catholic
and a non-Catholic meet in a truly brotherly spirit, each keeps
the formulation of faith which he considers to be authoritative.
The Catholic abstains from passing sentence on the other's
adhesion to what he himself holds to be errors. The non-
Catholic also suspends judgment as to the Catholic's conscien-
tious teaching of what he himself rejects. This is how things
should be. We all have a long way to travel before we can
usually behave in such a manner.

On the topic of practical charity among Christians of diverse
persuasions, the founder of the Methodist movement, John
Wesley, has a beautiful passage. In his "Letter to a Roman
Catholic" we find the following lines. They are worth quoting
extensively:

"O brethren, let us not still fall out by the way. I hope to
see you in heaven. And if I practise the religion above described, you dare not say I shall go to hell. You cannot think
so. None can persuade you to it. Your own conscience tells
you the contrary. Then if we cannot as yet think alike in all
things, at least we can love alike. Herein we cannot possibly
do amiss. For one point none can doubt a moment: God is
love, and he that dwells in love dwells in God and God in him.

"In the name, then, and in the strength of God, let us resolve, first, not to hurt one another; to do nothing unkind or
unfriendly to each other, nothing which we would not have
done to ourselves. Rather let us endeavor after every instance
of a kind, friendly and Christian behavior toward each other.

"Let us resolve, secondly, God being our helper, to speak
nothing harsh or unkind of each other. The sure way to avoid
this is to say all the good we can both of and to one another.
In all our conversation, either with or concerning each other,

to use only the language of love; to speak with all softness and tenderness; with the most endearing expression which is consistent with truth and with sincerity.

"Let us, thirdly, resolve to harbor no unkind thought, no unfriendly temper toward each other. Let us lay the axe at the root of the tree; let us examine all that rises in our heart, and suffer no disposition which is contrary to tender affection. Then shall we easily refrain from unkind actions and words when the very root of bitterness is cut up.

"Let us, fourthly, endeavor to help each other on in whatever we are agreed leads to the kingdom. So far as we can, let us always rejoice to strengthen each other's hands in God. . . . O, let you and me (whatever others do) press on to the prize of our high calling, that, being justified by faith, we may have peace with God through Our Lord Jesus Christ, by whom we have received the atonement." [6]

There cannot be a better practical program to foster peace among Christians. Only on those terms will our coexistence within one society actively prepare the final return of all to the unity given to the Church. How far we are from it, both in daily conduct and in thinking, is best left to each one to meditate. . . .

[6] Quoted in Harry Emerson Fosdick, *Great Voices of the Reformation* (1952), pp. 528f.

eight
Judaism as Challenge

A study of the relations between Catholics and Protestants leads to the germane problem of the Catholic attitude toward Jews. The issue is similar only to a certain extent. However mistaken they may be on some points of Catholic tradition, believers in Christ cannot be assimilated to men who do not acknowledge the Saviour. The similarity does not therefore lie in the nature of the faith involved. Protestants are relatively near to the Church. As individuals who have received baptism they are entitled to a special relation to her. Their communities themselves enjoy no such privilege. The situation of Jews is in sharp contrast to that. The Chosen People was entrusted with the Old Covenant. It received from God the promises. To it were the prophets sent. For centuries it maintained faith in the true God among world-wide paganism. It prepared and bore the Messiah as a woman bears her son. In as far as it survives today in the Jewish community, this People is now closely related to the Church. Individual Jews, however, share that relation in proportion as they also share the ancient faith of Israel, in the measure in which they are incorporated in the

Jewish people taken as a religious collectivity. Only from this standpoint.

As it follows, the attitude of Catholics toward Jews is to be carefully distinguished in theory from their conduct among Protestant Christians. Yet actual behavior in both cases ought to follow a like pattern. It should be pure charity. What differs is the doctrinal motive behind that behavior.

A fact needs to be emphasized: the Jewish religion is, from a Christian point of view, truly revealed. Historically and theologically the modern Synagogue is heir to the old pre-Christian Temple. True it is, the religious substance of Judaism has tended to dwindle step by step since the day when the last prophet, St. John the Baptist, came. In many individual cases it has indeed completely faded. Within faithful Judaism also there is no unity of doctrine. Several schools of thought (Orthodox, Conservative, Reformed) provide varying interpretations of the Jewish fact. Their unity is ensured by a common agreement on the unique importance of that fact and by a general fidelity to the Jewish cultural heritage. This is the part of man in the relation between God and Israel. As was to be expected it has evolved, with man himself. On the side of God, however, things remain unchanged. His promise to Abraham stands. The Church, admittedly, is heir to Abraham, the Father of the faith. Christians are, as Pope Pius XI said, "spiritually Semites." [1] Yet to this day and forever the Jews constitute the Chosen People to whom the Messiah belongs. Seen from a Christian standpoint, the Jewish situation is therefore twofold. In the first place, every Jew is a member of the People of Abraham. He shares the messianic vocation of his race, even if he renounces or ignores it. In the second, he partakes of this vocation more or less actually or at various

[1] Pius XI said this in September, 1938, when speaking to a group of Belgian pilgrims.

degrees of virtuality, according as he is more or less religious or skeptical. The former standpoint is that of God's calling. The latter is that of man's answer.

I have used the expression "messianic vocation" of the Jews. This perhaps calls for a word of explanation. Such a messianic vocation is not in question so far as ancient Israel is concerned. Up to the advent of Christ Jews were the messianic People. They expected the Messiah. Their prophetic books heralded His coming. In the words of St. Paul, "theirs are the sonship, the glory, the covenant, the giving of the Law, the service of God, the promises and also the Patriarchs." [2] The leaders of the Jewish people eventually rejected Christ. For their interpretation of the prophetic books did not fit the reality. In spite of this official condemnation of the Saviour, Jews have nevertheless kept their messianic vocation. This is clear in the passages of St. Paul's Epistle to the Romans, where the apostle defines the position of Israel. Apostasy, or rather blindness, has been permitted in order that the Church may have time to convert the pagans. This is the core of St. Paul's doctrine on the point. It is to be understood as regards Judaism as a whole. God did not blind individuals to the truth of the Messiah. He allowed only that the misunderstanding of a section of the people should provoke a collective "hardening of hearts." Paul successively belonged to both sides of the fence. He was in a position to know what fervor for the God of the Messiah motivated the refusal to acknowledge Jesus as the Christ. One can say with considerable evidence from the New Testament that the Jewish people was blinded by its religious zeal itself. However clear they may have seemed after the event, the messianic prophecies of the Old Testament seemed unavoidably ambiguous as long as they were unfulfilled. This was bound to cause trouble when the Messiah would come. Even after the event, the Church Fathers were far from one mind

[2] Romans 9:4.

as to the way in which Christ had fulfilled the Scriptures.[3] This radical ambiguity of the accomplishment of the Law by Christ acted as a stumbling block to not a few Jews of earnest religious convictions.

Be that as it may, the messianic vocation of Judaism has been transmitted down the centuries together with its religious zeal. This vocation may be understood today as a living token for Christians that the Messiah will return according to His promise. Jews among us have the mysterious role of pointing to the short time that we still have to bring pagans to Christianity. They remind Catholics that time will tell against them when the Day of Judgment arrives. For it will unveil all that could have been done and was not attempted. Judaism should inspire us with veneration for the ways of God and with anxiety. For while Jews fulfill their vocation of perpetuating fidelity to the Old Covenant, we may be neglecting ours of announcing the New.

On the last day Christ will "come into His own"[4] and, contrary to what happened the first time, His own will receive Him. According to St. Paul, the ultimate conversion to Christ of the Chosen People will mark the last period before the second and last coming of the Lord, at the end of the world. A few theologians favor a different interpretation of St. Paul's doctrine. As they see it, the conversion of Jews is not bound to take place in the last days of the world. When it does happen, it will only deepen the Church's life in what is called its eschatological dimension, that is, in the aspect of the Church that anticipates on eternity. The opposite view, however, seems to be better grounded in the Catholic tradition.[5]

If this is the Catholic view of Judaism, the actual comport-

[3] "Christianity and Israel: how did Christ fulfil the Law?" in *The Downside Review,* Winter, 1956–57, pp. 55–68.

[4] John 1:11.

[5] "Christianity and Israel: is the Church schismatic?" in *The Downside Review,* Autumn, 1955, pp. 347–58.

ment of many Catholics toward their Jewish neighbors is far from ideal. In this field, as in others, generalizations are hateful. One cannot say, in general, that Catholics are anti-Semites. Yet undoubtedly most are not fully aware of the religious vocation of Judaism in their midst. Rather than from Catholic doctrine, their attitude proceeds from social or racial prejudices. This anti-Semitism of Catholics is a theological monstrosity, located at the exact antipodes of the true connection between the Church and Israel. To no small extent, modern Catholics have inherited traces of the medieval attitude to Jews. With the disappearance of medieval society, these remains have been misinterpreted. They have lost their theological connotations. Unfortunately, they have also retained enough religious flavor to convey the false impression that a Catholic has to be, up to a point and in a certain sense, anti-Jewish.

The Middle Ages segregated Jews. These were relatively free within their ghettos. Some could even gain considerable influence outside. Jewish philosophy played no small role in the formation of scholasticism. The Talmud was in high favor during the fourteenth and fifteenth centuries at the beginning of the Renaissance. Rabbis were commonly consulted on points of Old Testament scholarship. Yet the location of Jewish quarters within Christian cities brought about pogroms, when ignorance and superstition made Jews the scapegoats of the people. At bottom, however, and in spite of these excesses, the medieval segregation of Jews proceeded from the identification then made between the Jewish people as a whole, heir to the Old Covenant, and each individual Jew. Just as Christianity, as faith, and Christendom, as civilization, were then coterminous, Judaism, as religion, and Jewry, as race, were also identified. The mind that made no distinction between Church and State among Christians would make none among Jews. This explains the status of Judaism as a state within the state during the Middle Ages. That was the medieval way of respecting the Jewish conscience. As conflicts between States arise easily, there were conflicts. Yet when the Spanish Inquisition, in 1492, expelled the Jewish communities to which Spain owed a great amount of its prosperity, it acted in keeping with the inner logic of the medieval conception of the State.[6] That the decision was immoral is another matter.

The medieval pattern has now changed. Yet the superstitious fear of Jews that was common in the Middle Ages has stayed on. It is all the deeper in the Christian mind as it can invent a theological justification. The falser this justification, the more obnoxious it grows. Bad theology always makes for superstition. In this case it is superstition that has created bad theology in order to give itself the illusion of a good conscience. The outcome is hard to undo. The idea that Jews are cursed because their ancestors crucified the Lord stands in contradiction to the Gospel. Christ excused His tormentors, Jews as well as pagans: "Father, forgive them: they know not what they do." [7] It is furthermore opposed to the Catholic doctrine on mankind's collective responsibility in sin. Those who put Christ to death were only the instruments of mankind as a whole. Since Christ died on account of our sins, we all are to blame for His crucifixion. Nevertheless, the idea is still often to be met with among people who are accounted good Catholics. To the mind of anti-Semitic bigots, it even explains a great deal of history. God would periodically "visit" the mur-

---

[6] Let us not be unfair to Spain. There had been an important precedent to the action of the Spanish monarchy. In 1290 King Edward I of England expelled all Jews from his kingdom. Only under Cromwell did the first Jews return. The decision of Edward I had purely mercantile motives. In its own action, the Spanish Inquisition was motivated by a despair of ever converting Jews: in 1414–1416, the "disputation" of Tortosa between rabbis and priests seemed to have exhausted the possibilities of conversion.

[7] Luke 23:34.

derers of Christ and incite them to penance through persecution. All the anti-Semitic excesses of times past and present can thus be cheaply excused. They are freely granted the blessing of Providence. And we, who have done so little or nothing to stop them, can rest satisfied in our religious arrogance.

I paint the picture at its worst, admittedly. But the worst does exist. It exists even in the United States, although the medieval pattern of relations between the Church and Israel never developed here. By a process which is common enough in American history, prejudices brought over from Europe have sometimes hardened on this side of the Atlantic while they softened on the older shore. In contact with a changed environment, some strata of American Catholic society have thus kept alive an anti-Semitism which is nowadays more rarely to be found in Europe. This is in no way an anti-Semitic doctrine. As a doctrine it could not live long within the Catholic communion. It is too much out of step with the essence of Catholicity for that. Undercurrents are, however, all the more dangerous as we can easily be persuaded of their non-existence.

Medieval anti-Semitism should indeed be regretted from a humanistic point of view. Its popular decay into superstition must be condemned from the standpoint of the Church herself. Its basis, however, had been essentially Christian. Its motive was specifically religious. For as it was then institutionalized, anti-Semitism respected the privilege status of Israel in the period inaugurated by the New Covenant. Although their mysterious origin and their nomadic way of life made them strangers to surrounding society, gypsies moved about freely. They had no distinct status. They were not hampered by a restrictive institution. Jews on the contrary were, on account of their religious vocation as interpreted by Catholic theology. In this way medieval anti-Semitism was a Catholic phenomenon. In keeping with St. Paul's view of religious history, it witnessed to the Catholic awareness of the sense of the Old Covenant and of the eschatological vocation of Jews.

The meaning of anti-Semitism in the modern world has completely changed. With the disappearance of medieval society, the religious value of Judaism has been lost to the prevailing secular mind. Jews had been given an ambiguous situation in Christian society. They reminded Christians of God's alliance with Abraham. They were living witnesses to the Church's expectation of the second coming of Christ. Jews also polarized the unreasoning fear of the masses. Now that society has ceased being Christian, the first aspect of Judaism has veered out of sight. Having lost this counterweight, the second aspect has waxed. Furthermore, our time has invented Jew baiting as a political creed. Once again anti-Semitism has been institutionalized. Instead of being based on a theological appraisal, it has fed on a pagan myth of blood brotherhood and race purity. Proposed as a theory long before Hitler was born, this anti-Semitic doctrine reached its peak of horror under the impulse of the German dictator. What took place in the Third Reich, however, was the outcome of centuries of decadence for which Christians are mostly responsible. The Nazi experience is over. Yet anti-Semitism is still linked with totalitarian ideologies. In spite of its professed belief in the equality of men, Russian Communism has fallen a prey to it. It is periodically fanned up in a number of Arab nations. When it tends to become exclusive, nationalism feeds on it. Instances of this can be borrowed from the history of any country.

The problem of anti-Semitism among Catholics is that these have also been marked by the secularization of modern life and thought. They have too, in numerous cases, lost sight of the spiritual nature of Israel. When and where they have professed anti-Semitism, they have simply adopted the standpoint of modern nationalists, which Christian theology, misunderstood or biased, covers up as an excuse. In good or in bad faith, the Gospel is then identified with purity of race, with citizenship understood in a narrow sense, with national tradition or way of life. Outside this professed anti-Semitism, which is fortunately on the wane, there also lingers a tenacious undergrowth of anti-Semitic feelings and assumptions. Medieval superstitions and many undue generalizations of unfortunate experiences feed one another in this. Jealousy, resentment, and a whole chain of psychological complexes keep it alive.

The first way to deal with anti-Semitism is to be aware of the troubled waters on which it thrives. Its distant origin in the medieval conception of society helps us to understand what spiritual decay was undergone before anti-Semitism became a political slogan. Once he is conscious of this, any honest Christian will react in the only possible way: atonement. Atonement implies making up for guilt. It also means bringing about union.

To the credit of the last decades a movement has originated among Catholics that favors a sounder approach to Judaism. The circle of Fr. Paul Démann in Paris, with its publication *Les Cahiers Sioniens,* has been active in this line for a long time. It tries to reinterpret the Jewish phenomenon from a Catholic point of view and in the light of recent developments in Jewish history. Professor Karl Thieme, in Switzerland and Germany, likewise attempts to draw out the full implications of the religious calling of Judaism. *Freiburger Rundbrief* is a periodical edited under his supervision. It is conceived as a sort of platform where problems of Judaism are discussed with reference to Catholic doctrine. In the United States Fr. John Oesterreicher and his Institute of Judeo-Christian Studies at

Seton Hall University have inaugurated a similar effort among American Catholics.[8]

The problem is to fight anti-Semitism. Only if we replace it by a positive doctrine and attitude can we defeat it. A condemnation of anti-Semitism, both as ideology and as feeling, must proceed from the depth of the Catholic position, from the religious involvement of the Catholic faith. For anti-Semitism ultimately denies the Jewish origin and ground of the Church. There is "neither Jew nor Greek" [9] in the Church only because she is the home of both Greek and Jew. This should foster a sort of ecumenical behavior of Catholics toward Jews. I myself use this word here only with misgivings. In its original meaning, "ecumenical" simply means Catholic. At the present time it also denotes the modern concern for Christian unity. There is a certain danger in using it in regard to non-Christians: the danger precisely of confusing issues, of seeing together problems that arise out of diverse data. Yet the practical behavior of Catholics toward Jews ought to be closely germane to the attitude to Protestants which an ecumenical-minded Catholic thought promotes. Karl Thieme has hit on the excellent expression of "diaconate," in its original connotation of "service." Christians ought to "serve" Jews in thanksgiving for the great service the Jewish people rendered the whole world when it prepared the ground for the Messiah. Service implies assistance in friendship.

An "ecumenical" approach to separated Christians is urged by their great number and the ensuing "scandal of divisions" among followers of Christ. A similar brotherhood with Jews is inspired by their providential place in the plan of Redemp-

[8] The Institute publishes a yearbook of Judeo-Christian studies, *The Bridge*. This title is a good summary of its aim.

[9] Gal. 3:28.

tion. The three phases of the Church's history (at the origin, now, and in the last days of the world) are to be understood by reference to Judaism. The Christians of the middle period, in which we are now living, bear a tremendous responsibility before Christ: to express in their daily life the kinship established between them and their elder brothers the Jews by the continuity from the Old to the New Covenant.